DEISM AND THE HUMAN JESUS

John H. Lindell

Edited by William Patterson

Kindle Direct Publishing

DEISM AND THE HUMAN JESUS. Copyright 2020 by John H. Lindell. All rights reserved. Printed in the United States of America. No part of this book may be reproduced or utilized in any form or by any means for commercial purposes without permission in writing from the author, John H. Lindell. Any request must be sent to: John H. Lindell, 2405 Rollingwood Drive, Austin TX 78746-5757 or email: Brojohn@austin.rr.com

Scripture quotations in this book are from the Revised Standard Version of the Bible, copyright 1946, 1952, and 1971 by the Division of Christian Education of the National Council of Churches of Christ in the U.S.A. Used by permission.

With permission of Oxford University Press, this book contains information from Documents of the Christian Church, second edition, selected and edited by Henry Bettenson, published in 1963.

Published by Kindle Direct Publishing, a subsidiary of the Amazon group of companies.

ISBN 9798663251778

Contents

EDITOR'S NOTE

This book was originally published on January 1, 2013 by John H. Lindell. Permission was given for an individual to print one copy from the author's website for the personal use of that individual. The book was on a PDF file and was designed to be printed on pages 8½ inches by 11 inches in size. It was recommended that the pages be put in a three-ring notebook or otherwise bound together. Permission was also given for an individual to print additional copies to be provided free of charge to other persons.

I had the privilege of contacting Brother John in emails in October and December 2016 and expressed my intention to visit with him in Austin where he lived. Unfortunately, events precluded any opportunity to see him. My own spiritual development had several similarities with his. Being born in 1931, I was baptized three times over the years, the first time in a river near Great Bend, Kansas. My reading interest in the historical Jesus began with the Quest described by Albert Schweitzer and continued through the majority of theology references throughout my life, more than 150 books in all. My presumably final beliefs are best characterized as Christian Deist.

I recently tried to renew a contact with John Lindell without success. His website is no longer active, he has not responded to emails and his phone is apparently disconnected. Videos can be located online with interviews and discussion of deism by Brother John, but these are already a few years old. Because the possibility exists that he has either passed away or is somewhere in a nursing facility, I have undertaken this project to publish his book as a permanent reference.

PREFACE

Deism is a natural religion that is known through human observation, experience, and reasoning. The English word "deism" comes from the Latin word "deus" which means "God." Deists believe that humankind originated intentionally, not accidentally. The intentional Originator is ordinarily called "God." Deists do not presume to describe God but infer the existence of God from the complex and purposeful designs found in the natural world and in human beings.

Natural religion is as old as humankind, but historically it acquired the name "deism" in the 17th century CE (Common Era or Christian Era) in England. At that time, religion was defined by the national Church of England in the Thirty-nine Articles of Religion adopted by the church in 1571. These Articles of Religion consisted of doctrines of trinitarian Christianity which were considered "orthodox." As the state religion, these doctrines were enforced by church and civil authorities. Anyone opposing these doctrines was subject to charges by the church and government, and might be imprisoned or executed.

Most of the early deists considered themselves to be "Christians" but they believed that the natural religion taught by the human Jesus had been subverted by the theology of Paul of Tarsus and revised in creeds created by a series of church councils beginning in 325 CE.

Deists view Jesus as a Jew who taught that true religion is based on the belief that one God is creator and ruler of the world, and that love for God and love for "neighbor" are God's basic laws (or "commandments") for humankind.

When Jesus was asked, "Which commandment (law of God) is first of all?" Jesus referred to the Hebrew Shema, "The first is, "Hear, O Israel: The Lord our God, the Lord is one; and you shall love the Lord your God with all your heart, and with all your soul, and with all your might" (Deuteronomy 6:4). The authors of the books of Matthew and Mark give slightly different wording (Matthew 22:34-38; Mark 12:28-30) but it is clear that Jesus is referring to the Hebrew Shema. God is to be loved (appreciated or valued) by a person in all that a person is, thinks, or does.

After Jesus said that the "first commandment" (law of God) is to love God, Jesus added, "The second is this, "You shall love your neighbor as (you love) yourself" (Mark 12:31). Jesus expanded the definition of "neighbor" to include everyone, even persons who were viewed as "enemies." In his teaching, Jesus went far beyond the definition of "neighbor" in Jewish religious law, at that time, which limited "neighbor" to Jewish neighbors and non-Jewish "sojourners" (guests) in the Jews' country (Leviticus 19:18,33-34).

How the simple religion of Jesus came to be the complicated and convoluted "orthodox" doctrines of the trinitarian Christian church is a story that most people do not know but need to learn if the deist movement is to be understood. Deists opposed such so-called "orthodox" doctrines as the trinity of God, the divinity of Jesus, "original sin" (from "Adam"), sacrificial atonement by Jesus' crucifixion, and unending torment for non-Christians in "hell." The deists intended to liberate the natural religion of Jesus from the entanglements of unreasonable theology that developed after the time of Jesus. Trinitarian church leaders viewed deism as a threat to the authority of the institutional church so deists became the targets of zealous attacks by trinitarian clergy.

To explain the rise of Deism in the 17th century, this book will begin with the story of Jesus and the development of "orthodox" trinitarian theology. Then we will review how some of the historical and intellectual developments in the world during sixteen centuries influenced the development of deism, and we will take a look at the deist leaders and writings that played prominent roles in the history of deism. Finally, we will look at deism, today, and its meaning for individuals who are interested in the practice of deism as a personal religion from a Christian Deist perspective.

But first, a reader has a right to know "where an author is coming from," so let me tell you about myself.

ABOUT THE AUTHOR

I was born in 1930. As a child, I grew up in Baptist churches where I was taught that everyone is naturally bad ("sinful") and will be punished by unending dying in a horrible place called "hell." I was told that the only way to avoid this punishment was to become a "Christian" by believing that God's only divine "Son" (Jesus) paid this death penalty for us by dying on a cross (crucifixion). At age 11, I became a "Christian" by "accepting Jesus as my savior." At age 14, I decided that I would become a Baptist preacher to save people from "hell."

At age 17, I entered Baylor, a Baptist university, as a ministerial student. Before then, I had not thought much about what I had been taught. In my sophomore year, I began to question the idea that people would go hell if they did not believe in "Jesus' sacrificial death on the cross." I recognized that most people in the world would never even hear about Jesus. It did not seem fair for God to treat people so unequally. Also, unending torture in hell seemed cruel. I could no longer accept these ideas.

After graduating from Baylor University, I got married, entered a Baptist theological seminary, and became pastor of a church in a small town. My experiences in the seminary and in the church led me to face the fact that I was not a Baptist in my beliefs, so I dropped out of the seminary and left the ministry to begin my search for what I could honestly believe.

I began a career in social work, obtained a master's degree in social work at the University of Texas, and spent 33 years in family and child social services. While my wife and I were rearing two sons and a daughter, we were members of Methodist churches, and I personally continued my search for what I could reasonably believe. At the age of 38, I wrote a small book entitled *Principles and Practice of Natural Religion* expressing my personal religious beliefs. I called my religion "Eso," a Greek word meaning "within" because I found my beliefs within myself from observation, experience, and reasoning.

In 1981, at age 50, I joined a Unitarian Church that belonged to the Unitarian Universalist Association (UUA). In its by-laws, the UUA stated that it would "cherish and spread the universal truths taught by the great teachers and prophets of humanity, immemorially summarized in the Judeo-Christian heritage as love to God and love to humanity." This described my personal religion. In 1985, the UUA deleted this statement from its by-laws because a majority of the members of UUA churches did not affirm a belief in God. Eventually, I realized that a UUA church was not the place for me.

In 1998, I discovered that my personal religion had been known as "deism" for more than 300 years. A deist named Matthew Tindal published a book, in 1730, entitled *Christianity as Old as Creation*: or, *The Gospel, a Republication of the Religion of Nature*. Tindal explained that belief in God and love for all people are the timeless principles of natural religion, and are the essence of "Christianity." Tindal used the term "Christian Deist" to refer to someone who holds this view. I am a Christian Deist.

HISTORICAL BACKGROUND

Jesus was a man who lived about two thousand years ago in a land just east of the Mediterranean Sea. Jesus was a Jew. To understand Jesus, he must be seen in his historical context.

According to their traditions, Jews believed that God had promised their ancestor, Abram (later called Abraham) that his descendants would become a great nation by which "all of the families of the earth shall be blessed" (Genesis 12:2-3).

The story is told in the book of Genesis in the Hebrew Bible. "The Lord appeared to Abram, and said to him, 'I am God Almighty, walk before me and be blameless. And I will make my covenant between me and you, and will multiply you exceedingly (Genesis17:1-2). . . . And I will establish my covenant between me and you and your descendants after you. . . . And I will give to you, and to your descendants after you, the land of your sojournings, all of the land of Canaan, for an everlasting possession; and I will be their God' "(Genesis 17:7-8). As a sign of this covenant, it was agreed that all of the male descendants of Abram (Abraham) would be circumcised.

Some of the descendants of Abraham, through his son Isaac and grandson Jacob (whose name was changed to "Israel") migrated to Egypt where their numbers multiplied. Israel's twelve sons were heads of families that became known as the "twelve tribes of Israel," or Israelites. The Israelites (also called "Hebrews") left Egypt, under the leadership of Moses, and eventually migrated back to the land of the Canaanites about 1,200 years before Jesus was born.

The twelve tribes of Israelites were eventually organized into a kingdom ruled by a succession of kings: Saul,

David, and Solomon. About 922 years BCE (Before Common Era or Before Christian Era), the kingdom divided into two kingdoms, known as "Judah" (two southern tribes) and "Israel" (ten northern tribes). Two hundred years later, in 722 BCE, Israel was conquered by the Assyrians. In 587 BCE, Judah was conquered by the Babylonians. Many of the Hebrew people were dispersed to other countries. The leading families of Judah were taken into exile in Babylonia.

When Persia conquered Babylonia, the Persian king Cyrus allowed the people of Judah to return to their homeland, in 538 BCE, and they began rebuilding their temple in Jerusalem. Nevertheless, the Jews continued to be ruled by Persia until being conquered by Alexander the Great from Greece in 332 BCE.

After the death of Alexander the Great, the Greek empire was divided among his four generals -- two of whom were Ptolemy, who ruled from Egypt, and Seleucus, who ruled from Syria. At first, the Jews were ruled by the Ptolemaic rulers from Egypt but in 198 BCE the Seleucid rulers from Syria took control over the Jews.

The Jews continued to hope that someday their nation, the Kingdom of Israel, would regain its independence in fulfillment of their expectation that the descendants of Abraham would be a great nation.

The Jews revolted against their Syrian ruler and gained their independence in 164 BCE. But after 101 years of independence, the Jews lost their freedom when the Romans took control of the Jews in 63 BCE.

Once again, the Jews began longing for their independence as a nation. Some Jews found hope in the book of Daniel which was written by an unknown Jewish writer near the time that the Jews obtained their freedom from Syria. The book encouraged the Jews to expect their freedom at that time. The book of Daniel describes a series of dreams that the Hebrew prophet Daniel allegedly had when the Jews were ruled by Babylon and were longing for their freedom then.

According to the book, in one of his dreams, Daniel saw "one like a son of man" who was given an everlasting kingdom by the "Ancient of Days" (God). The term "son of man" means "human being." The "son of man" in Daniel's dream, symbolized the Kingdom of Israel which was predicted to come. In the time of Jesus, the term "son of man" was sometimes used to refer to a leader (a "messiah" or "anointed one") who would be sent by God to re-establish the Kingdom of Israel (also called the "kingdom of heaven" or the "kingdom of God").

Based on their own interpretation of the book of Daniel, some Jews believed that the "son of man," or messiah, was due in Jesus' time. You can imagine the excitement when a man called John the Baptizer (or Baptist) appeared in the wilderness near the Jordan River and began preaching, "Repent, for the kingdom of heaven is at hand" (Matthew 3:2). Of course, those who heard John the Baptizer interpreted his message to mean that the time for liberation and restoration of the Kingdom of Israel was near.

The Jews believed that the fate of their nation depended on their obedience to God. Disobedience to God's commandments was considered "sin." John the Baptist called for the people to "repent" of their sins in preparation for the coming of the "kingdom" from God. Those who repented were baptized (immersed) by John in the Jordan River, symbolizing that their repentance had cleansed them from their guilt.

The message of John the Baptist was both religious and

political. The Jews did not separate religion from politics. John the Baptist was leading a religious-political movement to reestablish Israel as an independent kingdom. Jesus joined the movement when he asked John to baptize Jesus. John the Baptist thought that Jesus was the expected "messiah" who would liberate the Jews and reestablish the Kingdom of Israel.

KINGDOM OF GOD

As a Jewish revolutionary leader, John the Baptist was arrested and executed by Antipas, the puppet ruler appointed by the Roman emperor. "Now after John was arrested, Jesus came into Galilee, preaching the gospel of God, and saying, 'The time is fulfilled, and the kingdom of God is at hand; repent and believe in the gospel (good news)' (Mark 1:14-15). Jesus became the leader of the Jewish revolutionary movement which John the Baptist had started. Jesus was joined by other Jews including some of the followers of John the Baptist.

Originally, Jesus' concept of the "kingdom of God" was a nationalistic one, exclusively for the Jews. When Jesus sent his disciples out to preach the coming of the kingdom, Jesus told them "Go nowhere among the Gentiles (non-Jews), and enter no town of he Samaritans, but go rather to the lost sheep of the house of Israel (the Jews). And preach as you go, saying 'The kingdom of heaven is at hand' "(Matthew 10:5-7).

Also, in the beginning, Jesus viewed his mission in military terms. Jesus said, "Do not think that I have come to bring peace on earth; I have not come to bring peace, but a sword" (Matthew 10:34). There is no doubt that Jesus was a Jewish revolutionary who intended to liberate the Jews from their Roman rulers. The men who became followers of Jesus believed that they were joining a revolutionary movement to reestablish a Jewish "Kingdom of Israel" which they called "The kingdom of heaven" or the "kingdom of God."

But something very important happened. As Jesus moved about the countryside, announcing the coming of the "kingdom of God" and calling for repentance of sins in preparation for the kingdom, Jesus began describing a "kingdom of God" that would not be exclusively for the

Jews, nor would it come by military action. In the New Testament, there are about 30 parables (stories) by Jesus, and thirteen of them refer directly to the "kingdom of God." Jesus' new concept of the "kingdom of God" will be described in the next chapter of this book.

But for now, we must ask, "What influenced Jesus to change his concept of the "kingdom of God" and why is this important? There may be some clues in stories about Jesus in the synoptic gospels according to "Matthew, Mark, and Luke" in the New Testament.

As Jesus was preaching the coming of the Jewish "Kingdom of God," something began to happen. Jesus gained a reputation as a "healer." In the time of Jesus, it was believed that mental illness was caused by "demon possession." While Jesus was preaching, a mentally ill man caused a disturbance. Jesus said, "Be silent" and the man had a convulsion which the people interpreted as removal of an "evil spirit" from the man. The news of this "healing" spread fast, and people began coming to Jesus to be healed of diseases and disabilities (Mark 1:21-28).

Jesus tried to escape the crowds that were seeking healing, because this was distracting him from his mission of preaching the coming of the "Kingdom of God." Jesus said to his disciples, "Let us go to the next towns that I may preach there also, for that is why I came out" (Mark 1:38).

But the people continued to come for healing. In Gennesaret, "when the men of that place recognized him (Jesus), they sent round to all that region and brought him all that were sick, and besought him that they might touch the fringe of his garment; and as many as touched it were made well" according to the story written by an unknown writer about forty years later (Matthew 14:34-36). This was a time when scientific medical practice was unknown so superstitious beliefs about healing were widespread.

In the district of Tyre and Sidon, "a Canaanite woman from that region came out and cried (to Jesus), 'Have mercy on me, O lord (sir), son of David; my daughter is severely possessed by a demon.' But he (Jesus) did not answer her a word. And his disciples begged him, saying, "Send her away, for she is crying after us.' He (Jesus) answered (the woman), 'I was sent only to the lost sheep of the house of Israel (the Jews).' But she came and knelt before him, saying, 'lord (sir), help me.' And he (Jesus) answered, 'It is not fair to take the children's bread and throw it to the dogs.' She said, 'Yes, lord (sir), yet even the dogs eat crumbs that fall from their master's table.' Then he (Jesus) said to her, 'O woman, great is your faith! Be it done for you as you desire.' And her daughter was healed immediately" according to the story (Matthew 15:21-28).

In this story, we see a very human Jesus with a very common Jewish prejudice against Gentiles (non-Jews) in that day. Despite Jesus trying to ignore the woman, and even insulting her (as a Gentile "dog"), the woman persisted with her plea for help, and Jesus learned that this woman was a person of love and faith.

As Jesus traveled on his preaching mission, he had other encounters with persons of different nationalities and religions. Jesus met a Roman centurion (army officer in charge of 100 soldiers) who came to Jesus for help. "As he (Jesus) entered Capernaum, a centurion came forward to him, beseeching him, and saying, 'My servant is lying paralyzed at home, in terrible distress.' And he (Jesus) said, 'I will come and heal him,' But the centurion answered him, 'Lord (sir), I am not worthy to have you come under my roof; but only say the word, and my servant will be healed. For I am a man under authority, with soldiers under me; and I say to one, Go, and he goes and to another, Come, and he comes, and to my slave, Do this, and he does it.' When Jesus heard him (the centurion), he (Jesus) marveled, and said to him, 'Truly, I say to you, not even in Israel have I found such faith. I tell you, many will come from east and west and sit at table with Abraham, Isaac, and Jacob in the kingdom of heaven' "(Matthew 8:5-11)."And to the centurion. Jesus said, 'Go, be it done for you as you have believed.' And the servant was healed at that very moment" according to the story (Matthew 8:13).

Jesus also had an interesting encounter with a Samaritan. (Jews considered Samaritans to be of mixed race and unorthodox religion.) "On the way to Jerusalem, he (Jesus) was passing between Samaria and Galilee. And as he entered a village, he was met by ten lepers, who stood at a distance and lifted up their voices and said, 'Jesus, master (sir), have mercy on us.' When he (Jesus) saw them, he said to them, 'Go and show yourselves to the priests.' And they went and were cleansed (of leprosy). Then one of them, when he saw that he was healed, turned back, praising God with a loud voice; and he fell on his face at Jesus' feet, giving him thanks. Now he (the healed leper) was a Samaritan. Then said Jesus, 'Were not ten cleansed? Was no one found to return and give praise to God except this foreigner?' And he (Jesus) said to him (the Samaritan), 'Rise and go your way; your faith has made you well' (Luke 17:11-19).

The above stories were written by unknown writers forty years after the events allegedly happened so we have no verification that the healings actually occurred, but what we know is that as Jesus encountered persons of other nationalities, ethnic groups, and religions, Jesus' views became broader. The story of the Roman centurion is definitely linked to Jesus' new concept that the kingdom of God was not limited to the Jews. The stories of the Canaanite (non-Jewish) woman and the Samaritan leper also suggest that Jesus had a broadening appreciation for all people.

While these stories provide only anecdotal support for what may have changed Jesus' view of the 'kingdom of God" from a narrow nationalistic one achieved by military revolution, there is no doubt that Jesus' concept of the kingdom of God evolved into a different one.

Jesus told a number of parables in which he described a concept of the "kingdom of God' that is different from the traditional Jewish view of the "kingdom" which Jesus originally held.

Here is the parable of the "mustard seed" which is recorded in Matthew 13:31-32, Mark 4:30- 32 and Luke 13:18-19. The following is the parable as recorded in the book of Mark:

"And he (Jesus) said, 'With what can we compare the kingdom of God, or what parable can we use for it? It is like a grain of mustard seed, which, when sown upon the ground, is the smallest of all the seeds on earth; yet when it is sown it grows up and becomes the greatest of all shrubs, and puts forth large branches, so that the birds of the air can make nests in its shade.' "

Here is Jesus' parable of the "leaven" (Luke 13:20-21):

And again he (Jesus) said, 'To what shall I compare the kingdom of God? It is like leaven which a woman took and hid in three measures of meal, till it was all leavened.' "

Here is Jesus' parable of the "pearl" (Matthew 13:45):

"The kingdom of heaven is like a merchant in search of fine pearls, who, on finding one of great value, went and sold all that he had and bought it."

Here is Jesus' parable of the "hidden treasure" (Matthew 13:44):

"The kingdom of heaven is like a treasure hidden in a field, which a man found and covered up; then in his joy he goes and sells all that he has and buys the field."

The parables of the mustard seed, leaven, pearl, and hidden treasure certainly do not describe a political kingdom established by a military revolution. According to Jesus, the kingdom of God is planted like a mustard seed and grows into something useful. The kingdom of God is like leaven that has a permeating influence in what it is placed. The kingdom of God is like a fine pearl or hidden treasure that can be discovered.

Perhaps Jesus' new concept of the "kingdom of God" can be better understood from a conversation that Jesus had with some Pharisees. Jesus "being asked by the Pharisees when the kingdom of God was coming, he (Jesus) answered them, 'The kingdom of God is not coming with signs to be observed; nor will they say, Lo, here it is! or There! for behold, the kingdom of God is within you' "(Luke 17: 20-21). The Greek word translated "within" can also mean "among" or "in your midst." Either way, Jesus' concept of the "kingdom of God" appears to refer to a personal experience, not a political kingdom.

A Jewish scribe (scholar) asked Jesus, "Which commandment is first of all?" Jesus answered, "The first is, 'Hear O Israel; The Lord our God, the Lord is one; and you shall love the Lord your God with all your heart, and with all your soul, and with all your mind, and with all your strength." The second is this, 'You shall love your neighbor as yourself.' There is no other commandment greater than these." And the scribe said to him (Jesus), 'You are right, Teacher; you have truly said that He (God) is one, and there is no other (God) but Him; and to love Him with all the heart, and all the understanding, and with all the strength, and to love one's neighbor as oneself, is much more than burnt offerings and sacrifices." And when Jesus saw that he (the scribe) answered wisely, he (Jesus) said to him (the scribe), "You are not far from the kingdom of God." (Mark 12:28-34). It appears from this conversation that the kingdom of God is associated with love for God and love for neighbor.

Jesus said, "You have heard it was said, ' You shall love your neighbor and hate your enemy' but I say to you, Love your enemies and pray for those who persecute you, so that you may be sons of your Father who is in heaven; for He makes His sun rise on the evil and on the good, and sends rain on the just and the unjust" (Matthew 5:43-45). The meaning of this is clear: God loves (cares about) everyone, and it is God's will that we do likewise. The idea of "love your enemies" is certainly not a call for a military revolution.

According to Jesus, God's kingdom comes as God's will is done on earth (Matthew 6:10). Jesus summarized God's will for humankind as, "You shall love the Lord your God with all your heart, with all your soul, and with all your mind. This is the great and first commandment. And the second is like it, You shall love your neighbor as yourself" (Matthew 22:37-39).

Jesus uses the term "word of God" to refer to the "the commandment of God" (Mark 7:9-13). In his parable of the Sower, Jesus refers to the "seed" as the "word of God" (Luke 8:11) or "word" (Mark 4:14) or "word of the kingdom" (Matthew 13:19).

Here is the parable of the Sower according to the book of Matthew 13:3-9, 18-23):

"A sower went out to sow.and as he sowed, some seeds

fell along the path, and the birds came and devoured them. Other seeds fell on rocky ground, where they had not much soil, and immediately they sprang up, since they had no depth of soil, but when the sun rose they were scorched; and since they had no root they withered away. Other seeds fell upon thorns, and the thorns grew up and choked them. Other seeds fell on good soil and bought forth grain, some a hundredfold, some sixty and some thirty. He who has ears, let him hear" (Matthew 13:3-9).

"Hear then the (meaning of the) parable of the sower. When any one hears the word of the kingdom and does not understand (accept) it, the evil one comes and snatches away what is sown in the heart, and this is what is sown on the path.

"As for what was sown on rocky ground, this is he who hears the word and immediately receives it with joy; yet he has no root in himself, but endures for awhile, and when tribulation or persecution arises on account of the word, immediately he falls away.

"As for what was sown among thorns, this is he who hears the word, but the cares of the world and the delight in riches choke the word, and it proves unfruitful.

"As for what was sown on good soil, this is he who hears the word and understands it; he indeed bears fruit, and yields, in one case hundredfold, in another sixty, and in another thirty" (Matthew 13:18-23).

In the parable of the Sower, Jesus gives four examples of how individuals respond to the "word of God" which is "sown in the heart."

Some individuals reject God's word completely, like a hard path that will not allow seeds to take root. They let the temptation to do evil devour the truth, like birds devour seeds on the hard ground. In Jesus' day, the temptation to do evil was personified as the "evil one" (a tempter called Satan or the devil). This personification should not be taken literally but the temptation to do evil is real.

Other individuals initially accept God's law of love in a superficial way, like the thin, rocky soil receives the seed but when it becomes difficult to follow the way of love, they abandon it. They let truth wither away.

Other individuals let God's law of love get entangled and choked out by materialistic concerns, like thorny weeds prevent the seed from producing fruit.

However, some individuals accept God's law of love and produce fruits of love -- good deeds -- in various amounts. In the parable of the Sower, the "word of the kingdom" is "sown in the heart" but only "he (or she) who hears the word and understands (accepts) it, he (or she) indeed bears fruit (Matthew 13:23).

In the next two chapters, we will examine what it means to "love God" and "love your neighbor as yourself."

LOVE FOR GOD

Jesus summarized God's basic laws for humankind as, "You shall love the Lord your God with all your heart, with all your soul, and with all your mind. This is the great and first commandment. And the second is like it, You shall love your neighbor as yourself" (Matthew 22:37-39).

Before we can consider what it means to "love God," we must define the words "God" and "love."

First, let us consider the meaning of the word "God." As a person becomes aware of his or her own existence, it is normal to wonder, "How did I come into existence?" It is apparent that a person does not make any decision or take any action to bring his or her physical body or personal consciousness into being. This clearly implies that life comes from a source beyond ourselves.

Did the world and human life originate accidentally or intentionally? If human life originated accidentally then there is no inherent meaning or value in human life, and it would not matter how a person lives, or even whether a person lives or not. This pessimistic view of life does not appeal to most people.

The other choice is to believe that the world and humankind originated through the intentional actions of a "creator," usually called "God." No one can describe God but the existence of an intentional creator can be inferred from the complex and purposeful designs seen in the world and human beings. Ancient Greek philosophers viewed the design and order of the world as evidence of a "logos" or creative "Mind." The word "god" means "ruler," and God is viewed as the "ruler" or maker of natural laws by which the world and humankind are designed to operate.

Now let us consider the meaning of the word "love." Love means "to value" or "to appreciate." We love whatever we believe to be of "value" or "worth."

If you value your life and believe that it came from God, how shall you show your appreciation for the life you have received?

Jesus answers this question in his parable of the "Talents." The word "talent" refers to a kind of money in the time when Jesus lived. The parable is in Matthew 25:14-30, as follows:

"For it shall be as when a man going on a journey called his servants and entrusted to them his property; to one he gave five talents, to another two, and to another one, to each according to his ability. Then he went away.

"He who had received the five talents went at once and traded with them, and he made five talents more. So too, he who had two talents made two talents more. But he who had received the one talent went and dug in the ground and hid his master's money.

"Now after a long time the master of those servants came and settled accounts with them. And he who had received five talents came forward, bringing five talents more, saying, 'Master, you delivered to me five talents; here I have made five talents more.' His master said to him, 'Well done, good and faithful servant; you have been faithful over little, I will set you over much, enter into the joy of your master.'

"He also who had received the two talents came forward, saying, 'Master, you delivered to me two talents; here I have made two talents more.' His master said to him, 'Well done, good and faithful servant; you have been faithful over little, I will set you over much, enter into the joy of your master.'

"He who had received the one talent came forward, saying, 'Master, I knew you to be a hard man, reaping where you did not sow, and gathering where you did not winnow; so I was afraid, and I went and hid your talent in the ground. Here you have what is yours.' But his master answered, 'You wicked and slothful servant! You knew that I reap where I have not sowed and gather where I have not winnowed? Then you ought to have invested my money with the bankers, and at my coming I should have received my own with interest. So take the talent from him and cast the worthless servant into outer darkness, and there will men weep and gnash their teeth.' "

In the parable of the Talents, the servants (I will call them "employees") are loaned various amounts of money ("to each according to his ability") to invest and earn a profit for their master (whom I will call the "employer"). Two employees were "faithful" in investing the money and they were rewarded by the employer who promoted them to a greater job.

But the one employee made a feeble excuse for not investing his one "talent" by claiming that his employer was unfair ("reaping where you did not sow, and gathering where you did not winnow"). This employee ignored the fact that it was his duty to invest what had been entrusted him in order to produce something more. The employer provided the money to invest and it was the employee's job to do the "sowing and winnowing."

The employer took away the "one talent" from the unfaithful employee and fired him from his job.

In the parable, the first two employees did the best they could with what they had been given to invest. The employee with five talents produced five more, and the employee with two talents produced two more. Both employees received equal approval from their employer.

The parable of the Talents could be called the "parable of Life." In Jesus' parable, the employees were loaned various amounts of money to invest and produce more money as intended by their employer. Two of the employees used the money as intended. As they reported their actions, you can see their self-satisfaction in their accomplishments. They rewarded themselves with this feeling of self-satisfaction. They did not know that they would be rewarded with a job promotion by their employer. These two employees were just doing what was right to do.

In life, human beings are loaned various amounts of time, abilities, and opportunities for investment to produce something good in the world. Those who use this loan as intended will reward themselves with a feeling of self-satisfaction (called "happiness").

In Jesus' parable, the third employee refused to use what was loaned to him. He complained that the employer was unfair. That employee made no effort to do what he could do (invest the money with the bankers to draw interest). As a consequence, the employee lost his future with his employer.

In life, a person can complain that he or she did not get a fair share, and just refuse to do the best he or she could do with what he or she has received. We see individuals who become "drop-outs" in life. They waste their time and abilities, blame others, and wallow in self-pity or bitterness.

The failure to invest oneself as intended by God is disrespectful of God. This is clearly a failure to "love God."

The only way we can show our love for God is to use our time, abilities, and opportunities as God intends for us to use them.

So how does God intend for us to use our time, abilities, and opportunities? It is not a coincidence that Jesus connected God's commandments to "love God" and "love your neighbor as yourself." These are inseparable. Jesus said that the second commandment (love your neighbor as yourself) is "like" the first commandment (love God). They are two sides of the same coin. Love for God is shown by loving "your neighbor as yourself."

In the next chapter, we will consider what it means to "love your neighbor as yourself."

LOVE FOR NEIGHBOR

Each person is faced with the question, "How shall I live in relation to other people?" Jesus answered this question, "You shall love your neighbor as yourself" (Matthew 22:39.) This means "you shall love your neighbor as _you_ love yourself." From the design of human nature, it is natural for you to love (value) yourself. This "self-love" enables you to know when behavior is "right" or "wrong." Any action which is hurtful or uncaring toward you is instinctively recognized by you as "wrong," whether the action is by you or by someone else. Your power of reasoning tells you that behavior that is hurtful or uncaring to you is also "wrong" if done to other persons.

According to Jesus, "love your neighbor as yourself" means "whatever (good) you wish that others would do to you, do so to them" (Matthew 7:12; Luke 6:31). This has become known as the "golden rule" because its value is recognized by all reasonable persons. Its truth is validated by our own observation and experience, and it is the foundation of natural religion.

What is distinctive in the teaching of Jesus is his definition of "neighbor." As a Jew, Jesus had been taught to "love your neighbor as yourself" as stated in the book of Leviticus in the Hebrew Bible. Leviticus 19:18 states, "You shall not take vengeance or bear a grudge against the sons of your people, but you shall love your neighbor as yourself." Here, "neighbor" is defined as "sons of your own people" or, in other words, _your_ Hebrew (Jewish) neighbor. The only exception to this definition is made in Leviticus 19:33-34, "When a stranger sojourns with you in your land, you shall not do him wrong. The stranger who sojourns with you shall be as a native among you, and you shall love him as yourself; for you were strangers in the land of Egypt; . . ."

The book of Leviticus defines "neighbor" as "sons of your own people" (Leviticus 19:18) and "strangers who sojourn in your land" (Leviticus 19:33). In other words, "neighbor" only included persons who were Jews, or other persons who were temporarily in the Jews' country. There was no requirement for the Jews to love anyone else, and this was clearly demonstrated when Moses ordered the Hebrew army to slaughter or enslave people of other countries as the Hebrews marched through those countries on their way to invade the land of the Canaanites (Deuteronomy 20:10-17).

Jesus' definition of "neighbor" went far beyond the definition in the book of Leviticus. When Jesus said, "Love your neighbor," he was asked "Who is my neighbor?" (Luke 10:29). Jesus answered with the parable of the Good Samaritan, as follows:

"A man was going down from Jerusalem to Jericho, and he fell among robbers, who stripped him and beat him, and departed, leaving him half-dead. Now by chance a (Jewish) priest was going down that road; and when he (the priest) saw him (the wounded man), he (the priest) passed by on the other side (of the road). So likewise a Levite (another Jew), when he saw him (the wounded man), he (the Levite) passed by on the other side (of the road).

But a Samaritan, as he journeyed, came to where he (the wounded man) was; and when he (the Samaritan) saw him, he (the Samaritan) had compassion, and went to him and bound up his wounds, pouring on oil and wine; then he set him on his own beast and brought him (the wounded man) to an inn, and took care of him. And the next day, he (the Samaritan) took out two denarii (money) and gave them to the innkeeper, saying, 'Take care of him, and whatever more you spend, I will repay you when I come back.'

"(Then Jesus asked,) 'which of these three proved neighbor to the man who fell among the robbers?' He (a lawyer) said, 'The one who showed mercy on him.' And Jesus said to him, 'Go and do likewise' " (Luke 10:30-37).

In this parable, the man who was robbed and beaten was traveling "from Jerusalem to Jericho" (two cities in Judea). The implication of this geographical location is that the man who was robbed was a Jew (from Judea). The man who showed compassion on him was a Samaritan. This is significant because Samaritans and Jews generally did not like each other because of racial and religious differences. Each considered the other to be an "enemy."

The fact that, in the parable, a Samaritan had compassion on an "enemy" suggests than we should have compassion on anyone who is suffering, even those we consider to be an "enemy." Jesus said, "You have heard it said, 'You shall love your neighbor, and hate your enemy. But I say unto you, Love your enemies and pray for those who persecute you, so you may be sons of your Father who is in heaven; for He (God) makes his sun rise on the evil and on the good, and sends rain on the just and unjust" (Matthew 5:43-45). Of course, sunshine and rain are required to produce food to sustain human life. God cares about everyone, the just and the unjust.

In the parable, the Samaritan had compassion on an "enemy". This suggests that we should have compassion on anyone who is suffering. Jesus said, "Love your enemies, do good to those who hate you" (Luke 6:27). We usually consider our "enemies" to be those persons who have done something wrong to us or to someone we care about. "Love your enemies" does not mean that we should accept wrong behavior. It means that we should be ready to have compassion on anyone who suffers, even our "enemies" who hate us.

In his definition of "neighbor," Jesus included everyone.

In the parable of the Good Samaritan, we see two kinds of "failure to love." The robbers were deliberately "hurtful" toward the man who was robbed and beaten. The priest and Levite were deliberately "uncaring" because they were indifferent toward the suffering of the wounded man. Being "hurtful" or "uncaring" toward others are "failures to love" which are called "sin."

Since our Creator designed us to love (care about) each other, failures to love are contrary to the design of human nature, and bring self-judgment in normal persons of accountable age. Such wrong-doers are punished by feelings of self-condemnation (guilt) and loss of self-esteem. Relief from the distress of this punishment comes only if the wrong-doer repents of the sin.

In the next chapter, we will examine what is meant by "repentance."

REPENTENCE

When he preached the "gospel of God," Jesus said, "The time is fulfilled, and the kingdom of God is at hand," and then Jesus called for a response, "Repent, and believe in the gospel (good news)" (Mark 1:14-15). What does "repent" mean?

The meaning of "repent" is found in Jesus' parable of the Prodigal Son (Luke15:11-24), as follows:

"There was a man who had two sons, and the younger of them said to his father, 'Father, give me the share of the property that falls to me (by inheritance).' And he (the father) divided his living between them.

"Not many days later, the younger son gathered all that he had and took his journey to a far country, and there he squandered his property in loose living. And when he had spent everything, a great famine arose in that country, and he began to be in want.

"So he went and joined himself to one of the citizens of that country, who sent him into his fields to feed swine. And he would gladly have fed on the pods that the swine ate, and no one gave him anything.

"But when he came to himself he said, "How many of my father's hired servants have bread enough and to spare, but I perish here with hunger! I will arise and go to my father, and I will say to him, Father, I have sinned against heaven and before you; I am no longer worthy to be called your son; treat me as one of your hired servants.'

"And he arose and came to his father. But while he was yet at a distance, his father saw him and had compassion, and ran and embraced him and kissed him.

"And the son said to him, 'Father, I have sinned against heaven and before you; I am no longer worthy to be called your son.' But the father said to his servants, 'Bring quickly the best robe, and put it on him; and put a ring on his hand, and shoes on his feet; and bring the fatted calf and kill it, and let us make merry; for this my son was dead, and is alive again; he was lost and is found.' And they began to make merry."

The parable of the Prodigal Son illustrates the process and meaning of "repentance."

The process began when the young son recognized his wrong-doing against his father. The son had shown disrespect for his father by squandering the property that his father had given to him.

Next came the son's decision to turn away from (or stop) his wrong-doing and confess his sin with an attitude of contrition (feeling sorry for what he had done). The son said, "I will arise and go to my father, and I will say to him, 'Father I have sinned against heaven and before you. I am no longer worthy to be called your son. "Then came the son's actual change in direction in his life, and his confession of wrong-doing ("And he arose and came to his father . . . and the son said to him, 'I have sinned . . .' ").

The son's confession of sin was made to his father who had been hurt by the son's bad behavior, and the son was willing to make amends by working as a "hired servant."

The father's response was forgiveness and rejoicing ("For this my son was dead, and is alive again; he was lost and is found").

Some dictionaries define "repent" as "to feel sorry for sin and seek forgiveness." But the parable of the Prodigal Son shows that repentance is more than this. The process of repentance includes:

1. The recognition of sin and acceptance of personal responsibility for the sin (wrong-doing).

2. A sincere feeling of remorse and sorrow for having sinned.

3. A conscious decision to stop the wrong-doing.

4. An actual "turning away from" the sin. This is a change of direction in behavior.

5. A confession of sin and a humble request for forgiveness. This request for forgiveness is made to God and, if possible, is also made to the person who was hurt by the sin.

Repentance is not just an intellectual exercise of "feeling sorry" for sins. Repentance involves a "turning" of "reorientation" of one's life. The evidence of that change is seen in the "fruit." or how a person lives after repenting. John the Baptist told those who came to confess their sins that they must "bear fruit that befits (evidences) repentance" (Matthew 3:8).

Jesus said something else about repentance in the parable of the Unmerciful Servant (Matthew 18:23-35), as follows:

"Therefore the kingdom of heaven may be compared to a king who wished to settle accounts with his servants. When he began the reckoning, one was brought to him who owed him ten thousand talents (a large amount of money); and as he could not pay, his lord ordered him to be sold, with his wife and children and all that he had, and payment be made.

"So the servant fell on his knees, imploring him, "Lord, have patience with me, and I will pay you everything.' And out of pity for him the lord of that servant released him and forgave him his debt.

"But that same servant, as he went out, came upon one of his fellow servants who owed him a hundred denarii (a small amount of money); and seizing him by the throat he said, 'Pay what you owe.' So the servant fell down and besought him, 'Have patience with me, and I will pay you." He refused (to have patience) and went and put him in prison until he should pay his debt.

"When his fellow servants saw what had taken place, they were greatly distressed, and they went and reported to their lord all that had taken place.

"Then the lord summoned him and said to him, 'You wicked servant! I forgave you of all that debt because you besought me, and should not you have had mercy on your fellow servant, as I had mercy on you?' And in his anger his lord delivered him to the jailers, till he should pay all his debt."

Jesus said, "So also my heavenly Father will do to every one of you, if you do not forgive your brother from your heart."

Since this parable reflects a culture and time long ago when a person could be jailed for failure to repay a personal debt, we must ignore this outdated custom and focus on the meaning of the story.

The parable of the Unmerciful Servant teaches that God will forgive us in the same way that we are willing to forgive those who sin against us. In the prayer that Jesus taught his disciples to pray to God, Jesus makes this point: "And forgive us our sins, as we forgive those who sin against us" (Luke 11:4).

Jesus said, "If your brother sins, rebuke him, and if he repents, forgive him; and if he sins against you seven times in a day, and turns to you seven times, and says, 'I repent,' you must forgive him (Luke 17:3-4).

Again, Jesus said, "If you forgive men their trespasses, your heavenly Father will also forgive you, but if you do not forgive men their trespasses, neither will your Father forgive your trespasses" (Matthew 6:14-15).

It should be noted that Jesus introduced the parable of the Unmerciful Servant with the phrase "the kingdom of God may be compared to . . ." Then Jesus told this parable that focuses on "repentance and forgiveness." Jesus' concept of the kingdom of God is clearly related to repentance and forgiveness. According to Jesus, God forgives our sins if we repent and we forgive those who repent of their sins against us. There are no other requirements for obtaining God's forgiveness.

In his new concept of the "kingdom of God," Jesus taught that the "kingdom" comes as God's will is done on earth (Matthew 6:10). God's will is done when we love (care about) our neighbor (everyone) as we love (care about) ourselves. To deliberately cause human suffering or to deliberately be indifferent to human suffering is "sin" (failure to love), as illustrated in the parable of the Good Samaritan (Luke 10:30-37).

If we have chosen to follow God's natural law of love that is "sown in the heart," we will experience remorse and sorrow whenever we fail to love. This will lead us to repent (turn away from) such unloving behavior and seek forgiveness Repentance is evidence that a person is sincerely committed to living as God intends for us to live.

If a mentally competent adult is not committed to following God's natural law of love, such person will not feel any remorse or sorrow over a failure to love. Without repentance, there is no forgiveness for such person. Repentance is an essential part of Jesus' message about the "kingdom of God." After Jesus survived his crucifixion, he met with his disciples and told them that "repentance and forgiveness of sins should be preached to all nations" (Luke 24:47).

GOSPEL

The word "gospel" means "good news." In the book called the New Testament, there are two different messages called "the gospel." One was given by a man called Jesus of Nazareth, and the other was given by a man called Paul of Tarsus.

The gospel given by Jesus is that the "kingdom of God" (the reign of God) comes on earth when people follow God's commandments (laws) to "love God" and "love your neighbor as yourself." Love for God is shown by love for neighbor. Sin is failure to love (by causing human suffering or by being indifferent to human suffering). God's forgiveness of sin comes when a person repents of sin. Repentance is evidence that a person is sincerely committed to trying to follow God's law of love for neighbor. Following the way of love brings life that Jesus called "abundant." This is the gospel that Jesus preached.

Paul of Tarsus preached a different "gospel." Paul was a Jew who believed that God imposed a death penalty on humankind because of sin (disobedience to God), beginning with the "first man" (Adam) who disobeyed God, (according to the story in the book of Genesis in the Hebrew Bible). Paul believed that Jesus was God's divine Son who became a human being so he could die as a sacrifice to pay the death penalty on behalf of humankind. Paul claimed that God raised Jesus from the dead and made him "lord" (ruler) of all humankind. According to Paul, if a person accepts Jesus as "lord" and believes that God raised him from the dead, that person would be given life after death.

What you usually hear in churches and on TV and radio today is Paul's "gospel." Who was Paul? How did his "gospel" come into being? How did it become dominant in Christian churches today?

Paul, whose Jewish name was Saul, lived during and after the time of Jesus. Paul never claimed to have seen Jesus or heard Jesus except in some kind of "vision" after the death of Jesus. From this "vision" of Jesus, Paul became convinced that Jesus was the "messiah" ("christos" in Greek) who would become ruler ("lord") of all humanity, not just the "kingdom of Israel."

Paul claimed to belong to the Jewish sect of the Pharisees. The writer of the book of Acts of the Apostles wrote that Paul was a Roman citizen and he had studied under the Jewish teacher Gamaliel in Jerusalem. The writer of Acts also wrote that Paul was from the city of Tarsus. Tarsus was the capital of the province of Cilicia which was in the southeastern part of Asia Minor, as it is now known. Tarsus was a city with a "Hellenized" (Greek) culture.

Initially, Paul viewed the followers of Jesus as heretical for claiming that Jesus was the Jewish messiah. Religious officials gave Paul authority to arrest the followers of Jesus in the city of Damascus. On his way to Damascus, Paul had some kind of "vision" of Jesus that convinced Paul that Jesus was the messiah ("christos") expected by the Jews.

The English word "Christ" in the New Testament is a transliteration of the Greek word "christos" (a verbal adjective meaning "anointed") which, in turn, is a translation of the Hebrew word "mashiach," a participle which also means "anointed"). "Mashiach" refers to someone who has been chosen for a special purpose, like a king who may be "anointed" with oil in a coronation ceremony. The Jews expected a mashiach who would become their king. Mashiach is "messiah" in English.

The followers of Jesus called him the "christos" (Christ)

and eventually they became known as "Christians." In his letters to early churches, Paul often referred to Jesus just by the title "christos" (Christ).

What did Paul believe about Jesus, and how did many of Paul's ideas become dominant in Christian churches?

Although Paul considered Jesus to be God's divine Son, "in the form of God" (Philippians 2:6), Paul believed that Jesus was subordinate to God whom Paul called "the Father." Paul wrote, "Yet for us there is one God, the Father, from whom are all things and for whom we exist, and one lord, Jesus Christ, through whom are all things and through whom we exist" (I Corinthians 8:6). "When all things are subjected to him (Jesus), then the Son himself will also be subjected to Him (God) who put all things under him (Jesus), that God may be everything to everyone" (I Corinthians 15:28). As explained previously, Paul used the term "lord" to mean the one chosen by God to rule all humanity.

As indicated above, Paul believed that Jesus was the means by which God "the Father" created "all things" including humankind. Paul's belief reflects the influence of Greek philosophy. The Greek philosopher Heraclitus (600 years before Paul) believed that a "logos" (creative intelligence or "mind") created the order of the world. Greek ideas, such as this, would have been known in Paul's hometown of Tarsus.

The concept of the "logos" is seen also in the Gospel According to John a book written more than 30 years after Paul's time. The unknown writer of the book of John stated that the "logos" was "in the beginning with God" and "all things were made through him (the logos)" (John 1:2). The writer added, "And the logos became flesh and dwelt among us, full of grace and truth; we have beheld his glory, glory of the only Son of the Father." This, of course, refers to Jesus as the Son of God.

Paul began preaching that Jesus was the "messiah" (Christ) whom the Jews were expecting but Paul immediately ran into a problem. The Jews were not expecting a messiah to be crucified. According to the book of Acts, Paul "came into Thessalonica where there was a synagogue of the Jews. Paul went in, as was his custom, and for three weeks he argued with them from the (Hebrew) scriptures, explaining and proving that it was necessary for the Christ to suffer and rise from the dead, and saying, 'This Jesus, whom I proclaim to you, is the Christ" (Acts 17:1-3).

Paul's theory about why Jesus had to die is explained in Paul's letter to the Christians in Rome. Paul used the story of "Adam and Eve" in the Hebrew book of Genesis to explain the origin of sin and death. "Therefore sin came into the world through one man (Adam) and death through sin, so death spread to all men because all men sinned" (Romans 5:12). Then Paul wrote that people are saved from sin and death by Jesus' death on the cross (his crucifixion). "But God shows his love for us in that while we were yet sinners Christ (Jesus) died for us. Since therefore we are now justified by his blood, much more shall we be saved from the wrath of God" (Romans 5:8-9). Paul believed that Jesus' death was a blood sacrifice to atone for sins.

Paul's idea of atonement by sacrifice came from Jewish religious beliefs. In the time when Paul lived, the Jews had a complicated sacrificial system in their religion. The book of Leviticus in the Hebrew Bible describes the kinds of sacrifices that were offered in the Jewish temple at Jerusalem to "atone" for sins committed knowingly and unknowingly.

For sins committed knowingly against one's neighbor,

restitution was required and a "ram (male sheep) without blemish" was sacrificed in the temple as a guilt offering "to make atonement for him (the sinner) before the Lord, and he (the sinner) shall be forgiven for any of the things which one may do and thereby become guilty" (Leviticus 6:6-7).

The offering of a sacrifice was considered an act of obedience to God. Paul used this "sacrifice" analogy to interpret Jesus' crucifixion as an act of obedience to God to atone for the sins of humankind. Paul wrote, "For as by one man's (Adam's) disobedience many were made sinners, so by one man's (Jesus') obedience many will be made righteous" (Romans 5:19).

According to Paul, "Christ Jesus, who though he was in the form of God, did not count equality with God a thing to be grasped (claimed), but emptied himself, taking the form of a servant, being born in the likeness of men. And being found in human form, he humbled himself and became obedient unto death, even the death of the cross. Therefore God has highly exalted him and bestowed on him the name (authority or status) which is above every name, that at the name of Jesus every knee should bow, in heaven and on earth, and every tongue confess that Jesus Christ is lord (ruler), to the glory of God the Father" (Philippians 2:5-11).

Paul concluded that salvation from sin and death comes to individuals who accept Jesus as "lord" and believe in the resurrection of Jesus. Paul wrote, "Because if you confess with your lips that Jesus is lord, and believe in your heart that God raised him from the dead, you will be saved" (Romans 10:9).

The idea that Jesus was "sinless" came from Paul. Paul wrote, "For our sake He (God) made him (Jesus) to be (a sacrifice for) sin who knew no sin, so that in him we might become the righteousness of God" (2 Corinthians 5:21). A later writer in the book of First Peter (in the New Testament) referred to Jesus as a sacrificial "lamb without blemish or spot." "You know that you were ransomed from the futile ways of your fathers, not with perishable things such as silver or gold, but by the precious blood of Christ, like that of a lamb without blemish or spot." (First Peter 1:18-19). This is clearly a reference to the sacrifice of a "ram without blemish" described in the Hebrew book of Leviticus (6:6).

Paul called his gospel the "gospel of Christ" (Romans 15:19). Paul summarized his "gospel" in his letter to the Christians at Corinth, "Now I would remind you, brethren, in what terms I preached to you the gospel, which you received, in which you stand, by which you are saved, if you hold it fast -- unless you believed in vain. For I delivered to you as of first importance what I also received, that Christ died for our sins in accordance with the scriptures, that he was buried, that he was raised on the third day in accordance with the scriptures, and that he appeared to Cephas (Peter), then to the twelve. Then he appeared to more than five hundred brethren at one time, most of whom are still alive, though some have fallen asleep (died). Then he appeared to James and to all of the apostles. Last of all, as to one untimely born, he appeared also to me" (I Corinthians 15:1-8).

How did Paul get the "gospel" that he preached? In his letter to the Christians in Galacia, Paul wrote, "For I would have you know, brethren, that the gospel which was preached by me is not man's gospel. For I did not receive it from man, nor was I taught it, but it came through a revelation of Jesus Christ" (Galatians 1:11-12). Paul claimed that his "gospel" came to him by a supernatural revelation from Jesus after Jesus' death. The problem with Paul's claim is that his "gospel" is totally different from what Jesus preached, according to the books of Matthew,

Mark, Luke, and John. According to those books, Jesus never claimed that he came to die as a sacrifice to atone for the sins of humankind, and Jesus never asked his disciples to preach this.

Paul preached his "gospel" in Asia Minor and Greece. He had little success in his efforts to convince the Jews that Jesus was the messiah, but Gentiles (non-Jews) were attracted to Paul's claim that eternal life could be obtained by accepting Jesus as "lord" and believing in his resurrection from the dead. Paul believed that Gentiles could become Christians without converting to Judaism with its requirements of circumcision for males, and dietary laws for all. Paul preached that God had designated Jesus as "lord" over all, both Jews and Gentiles.

Paul preached that the world, as it was, would soon come to an end when Jesus returned to destroy all evil, and give eternal life to Christians. Paul wrote the following:

"I mean, brethren, the appointed time has grown very short; from now on, let those who have wives live as though they have none, and those who mourn as though they are not mourning, and those who rejoice as though they are not rejoicing, and those who buy as though they had no goods, and those who deal with the world as though they had no dealings with it. For the form of this world is passing away"(I Corinthians 7:29-31).

Paul wrote, "For in Adam all die, so also in Christ shall all be made alive. But each in his own order: Christ the first fruits, then at his coming those who belong to Christ. Then comes the end, when he (Jesus) delivers the kingdom to God the Father after destroying every (evil) rule and every (evil) authority and power. For he (Jesus) must reign until he has put all his enemies under his feet. The last enemy to be destroyed is death" (I Corinthians 15:22-26).

Paul also wrote, "But we would not have you ignorant, brethren, concerning those who have fallen asleep (died), that you may not grieve as others who have no hope. For since we believe that Jesus died and rose again, even so, through Jesus, God will bring with him those who have fallen asleep (died). For this we declare to you by the word of the Lord, that we who are alive, who are left until the coming of the Lord, shall not precede those who have fallen asleep (died). For the Lord himself will descend from heaven with a cry of command, with the archangel's call, and with the sound of the trumpet of God. And the dead in Christ will rise first; then we who are alive, who are left, shall be caught up together with them in the clouds to meet the Lord in the air; and we shall always be with the Lord. Therefore comfort one another with these words" (I Thessalonians 4:13-18). Paul believed that Jesus would return to the earth during Paul's lifetime.

We know now that that this did not happen. It is generally believed that Paul died between 60 CE and 65 CE, probably in Rome where Paul was under house arrest. Paul preached his "gospel" for about 30 years in Asia Minor and around Greece. His followers formed "house churches" to which Paul wrote letters of instruction. Some of these letters are found in the New Testament and have propagated Paul's views concerning Jesus through the centuries.

In 66 CE, the Jews revolted against their Roman rulers in an effort to liberate the kingdom of Israel from the Roman Empire. The Christians in Jerusalem saw what was happening and some fled across the Jordan River to Pella and other places. In 70 CE, the Romans crushed the revolution, devastated Jerusalem, and destroyed the Jewish temple. Jerusalem had been the headquarters for the disciples closest to Jesus, such as Peter, James and others, who still considered themselves to be Jews in a messianic sect in Judaism.

After the destruction of Jerusalem, the influence of the Jewish Christians began to decline. The churches in Asia Minor, Greece, Rome, and other places, where Paul had spread his "gospel," took over leadership in the Christian movement. Paul's theology was dominant in those churches.

One of Paul's ideas caused much debate among church leaders. Although Paul believed that Jesus was "in the form of God" (Philippians 2:5) and was the "Son of God," Paul believed that Jesus was subordinate to "God the Father" (I Corinthians 8:6; 15:28). If the "Father" and the "Son" were both divine but one ranked lower than the other, this sounded like "two Gods" or polytheism (belief in more than one God).

To refute the accusation that they were polytheists, various church leaders tried to explain how Jesus related to "God the Father." This question was debated by church leaders for three centuries. There were charges and counter-charges of "heresy" against each other. Eventually, a church council was called in 325 CE to settle the question by writing an "orthodox" Christian creed.

In the centuries that followed, many church councils were held and many creeds developed. Many of the beliefs held in churches today came from those creeds. As a background for understanding the rise of Christian deism, those church creeds will be examined in the next chapter.

CREEDS

In the fourth century CE, under the Roman emperor Constantine, Christianity became an officially recognized religion in the Roman Empire. Constantine became concerned that theological controversy about the relationship of Jesus to "God the Father" would be disturbing to the unity and stability of the empire. So Constantine called the church leaders together in a Council at Nicaea in 325 CE to settle the debate.

At that time, a Christian priest named Arius in Alexandria, Egypt, was preaching that Jesus was divine because he had been <u>created</u> by God the Father before the world was created but that Jesus was <u>subordinate</u> to God the Father. Arius' view became known as "Arianism." Arius' bishop, Alexander, and the theologian Athanasius argued that Jesus was <u>co-eternal</u> (had always existed) and had <u>equality</u> with God the Father.

After a long and bitter debate at the Council of Nicaea, the view held by Alexander and Athanasius prevailed and was adopted by the Council which produced a written creed, as follows:

"We believe in one God the Father All-sovereign, maker of all things visible and invisible;

"And in one Lord Jesus Christ, the Son of God, begotten of the Father, the only begotten, that is, of the <u>substance</u> of the Father, God of God, Light of Light, true God of true God, begotten, <u>not made</u>, of one <u>substance</u> with the Father, through whom all things were made, things in heaven and things on earth; who for us and for our salvation came down and was made flesh, and became man, suffered and rose on the third day, ascended into the heavens, is coming to judge the living and dead.

"And (we believe) in the Holy Spirit.

"And those that say 'There was (a time) when he (the Son) was not (in existence),' and 'Before he (the Son) was begotten he was not (in existence),' or that 'He (the Son) came into being from what-is-not.' or those that allege, that the Son of God is 'Of a different substance or essence' or 'created' or 'changeable' or 'alterable,' these the Catholic and Apostolic Church anathematizes (denounces)."

This creed claimed that the "Son of God" was not created by "God the Father" but was "begotten" (born) from God the Father. It also claimed that the "Son" existed as one "substance" with the "Father" before the "Son" was begotten by God, so the Son was "true God of true God." In this way, this creed tried to refute the accusation that the Son and the Father were two separate Gods (polytheism).

This creed also claimed that the Son was the means by which the world was created, indicating that the Son was begotten in heaven before the creation of the world. Then the creed claimed that the Son came down (from heaven to earth) "for our salvation" and "became man (Jesus), suffered (death) and rose on the third day, ascended into the heavens, is coming to judge the living and dead." This creed, produced by the Council of Nicaea, obviously reflects the position taken by bishop Alexander and theologian Athanasius who believed that the terms "Son of God" and "God the Father" refer to one God, not two. This means that "Jesus" is just another name for God. The terms "Jesus" and "God" are used synonymously and interchangeably in sermons and hymns in trinitarian Christian churches today.

However, the creed produced by the Council of Nicaea (325 CE) did not really settle anything. The debate continued about the relationship of Jesus to "God the

Father." Another church council met in Antioch in 341 CE and wrote a rather ambiguous creed that could be interpreted that the "Son" and "God the Father" were co-eternal but had different "personalities" and held different "ranks." This creed was acceptable to the Arian churches in the East, but the Western bishops held a council in Sardica in 343 CE supporting the Council of Nicaea creed of 325 CE.

In 344/345 CE, another church council at Antioch produced a creed that sounded like the Council of Nicaea creed but allowed for an Arian interpretation. In 357 CE, a council at Sirmium adopted an Arian creed that stated that the "Father" was greater than the "Son," but this creed was opposed by a church council at Ancyra in 358 CE. Another church council at Sirmium in 359 CE produced a creed that was more of compromise but in 381 CE a council at Constantinople reaffirmed the 325 CE creed from Nicaea.

The Council of Constantinople did not leave a record of the creed in 381 CE but the following creed came to be used generally in the churches after that date, and was affirmed by a church council at Chalcedon in 451 CE. The creed from Constantinople became known as the "Nicene Creed" because it was based on the 325 CE creed from Nicaea but substantial additions and modifications were made to the 325 CE creed.

This "Nicene Creed" became the "orthodox" creed in trinitarian churches and is recited in some churches today. The creed is as follows:

"We believe in one God the Father All-Sovereign, maker of heaven and earth, and of all things visible and invisible.

"And in one Lord Jesus Christ, the only-begotten Son of God, begotten of the Father before all ages, Light of Light, true God of true God, begotten <u>not made</u>, of one substance with the Father, through whom all things were made; who for us men and our salvation came down from the heavens, and was made flesh of the Holy Spirit and the Virgin Mary, and became man, and was crucified under Pontius Pilate, and suffered and was buried, and rose again on the third day according to the Scriptures, and ascended into the heavens, and sitteth on the right hand of the Father, and cometh again with glory to judge the living and dead, of whose kingdom there shall be no end;

"And in the Holy Spirit, the Lord and Life-giver, who proceedeth from the Father, who with the Father and Son is worshipped together and glorified together, who spake through the prophets;

"(And) in one Holy and Apostolic Church. We acknowledge one baptism unto the remission of sins.

"We look to the resurrection of the dead, and the life in the age to come."

The "Nicene Creed" officially created the church doctrine of the "Trinity" of God as "Father, Son (Jesus), and Holy Spirit" who are "worshipped together." This creed also included the doctrine that "remission of sins" came through baptism. Since baptism was a function controlled by the church, the church claimed to have the power to decide who would have "salvation" from sin and death. This gave the Catholic church enormous power over its members, including leaders of governments.

The western churches (under the leadership of the church at Rome) and the eastern churches (under the leadership of churches at Constantinople, Antioch, Jerusalem, and Alexandria) gradually drifted apart and split in 1054 CE when the church at Rome tried to assert leadership over all churches through a pope at Rome.

In the sixteenth century CE, the Protestant Reformation began in the Western church which had become known as the Roman Catholic Church. ("Catholic" means "universal.") The Protestant Reformation produced innumerable Christian sects which wrote their own creeds or statements of belief.

Although there are significant differences in the beliefs held by various Christian sects, Paul's belief that Jesus died on a cross as a sacrifice to save sinners from a death penalty was accepted in the Roman Catholic and Protestant churches. Paul's belief that Jesus was divine ("in the form of God") but subordinate to "God the Father" contributed to a controversy that eventually led church councils to develop the doctrine of the "Trinity of God" to refute the accusation of polytheism.

Athanasius, a major architect of the creed of Nicaea (325 CE) adopted Paul's doctrine of salvation coming through the death of Jesus. Believing that death is the penalty for sin, Athanasius wrote, "What then ought God do about the matter? Demand repentance . . .? But this would not safeguard the honor of God's character, for He would remain inconsistent if death did not hold sway over man . . . What else was needed (to save humankind) . . . but the Logos of God. . . . The Logos takes on a body (Jesus) capable of death, in order that, by participating in the Logos, it might be worthy to die instead of all (humankind) . . . Hence he (Jesus) did away with death for all who are like him by offering a substitute. For it is reasonable that the Logos, who is above all, fulfilled the liability in (by) his death, and thus the incorruptible Son of God . . . naturally clothes all (believers) with the incorruption in promise concerning the resurrection (from death)."

It is clear that Athanasius adopted Paul's theory of

salvation that is called the "substitutionary theory of atonement." In this theory, Jesus substituted his death to pay the death penalty which humankind had incurred by sin (disobedience to God). According to Paul and Athanasius, repentance from sin was not enough to obtain God's forgiveness. Paul's and Athanasius' theory is contrary to what Jesus said about repentance and forgiveness, in Chapter Five above. As seen in the Nicene Creed (381 CE), the Catholic church taught that water baptism was required for remission of sins. Since baptism is a function performed by the church, this gave Christian clergy control over who could be "saved." The church taught that infants inherited guilt from "Adam's original sin" and were condemned to "hell" from the time of birth unless baptized by a Christian priest.

The theology of the Nicene Creed was carried over into Lutheran churches in the sixteenth century CE. The Lutheran Augsburg Confession of 1530 states:

"We unanimously hold and teach, in accordance with the decree of the Council of Nicaea, all men are full of evil lust and indications from their mothers' womb   Moreover, this inborn sickness and heredity sin is truly sin and condemns to the eternal wrath of God all those who are not born again through Baptism and the Holy Spirit. . . .God the Son became man   was crucified, died and buried in order to be a sacrifice not only for original sin but for all other sins and to propitiate God's wrath. . . It is taught among us that Baptism is necessary and grace is offered through it. Children, too, should be baptized, for in Baptism they are committed to God and become acceptable to him."

During the Protestant Revolution, the "Reformed" churches led by John Calvin, Ulrich Zwingli, and others, differed in some respects from the Lutheran churches, led by Martin Luther, but the Reformed churches accepted trinitarian theology and Paul's theory of salvation through the death of Jesus.

An "anti-trinitarian" movement also began in the sixteenth century CE and was opposed by the Roman Catholic Church and the Protestant churches led by Martin Luther and John Calvin. The anti-trinitarian movement was led by Michael Servetus of Spain, Francis David of Transylvania, and Faustus Socinus of Italy.

The anti-trinitarians viewed Jesus as subordinate to God "the Father," but there was no agreement among them about the identity of Jesus. Michael Servetus (1511-1553) believed that God was Jesus' father but that Jesus did not exist before he was born on earth, so Jesus was separate from God and subordinate to God. Francis David (1510-1579) believed that Jesus was "begotten in the womb of the virgin (Mary) by the Holy Spirit," and that Jesus did not exist before his birth on earth. Francis David believed that Jesus was both "God and man." Faustus Socinus (1539-1604) believed that Jesus was a "true man by nature" but not a "mere man" because he was "conceived by the Holy Spirit and born of the Virgin Mary."

John Biddle (1615-1662), a Unitarian (anti-trinitarian) in England, taught that Jesus had "no other than a human nature." Theophilus Lindsey (1733-1804), who organized the first Unitarian congregation in England, believed that Jesus was a "man of the Jewish nation." Thomas Belsham (1750-1829) of England believed in the "unity of God and the simple humanity of Jesus Christ."

In 1819, the American minister William Ellery Channing preached his famous sermon entitled "Unitarian Christianity" in which he admitted that there were various opinions among Unitarians about Jesus, but there was agreement that Jesus' death was not necessary to save people from the penalty for sin. Channing said that God is always ready to forgive those who repent of sin. In 1825, six years after Channing's sermon, the American Unitarian Association was formed.

American Unitarianism became an organized denomination in 1865 with the formation of the National Conference of Unitarian Churches that identified itself as consisting of "Christian Churches of the Unitarian Faith."

In 1894, a statement by the National Conference affirmed that "These Churches accept the religion of Jesus, holding in accordance with his teaching, that practical religion is summed up in love for God and love to man" but that "Nothing in this Constitution is to be construed as an authoritative test; and we cordially invite to our working fellowship any who, while differing from us in belief, are in general sympathy with our practical aims."

In effect, Unitarian churches became "non-creedal" organizations. During the early 1900's, the Unitarian Christians became outnumbered by those members who differed from them "in belief," especially by non-theist humanists who appreciated the humanitarian "aims" of Unitarian Churches but affirmed no belief in God.

In 1961, the American Unitarian Association merged with the Universalist Church in America to form the Unitarian-Universalist Association (UUA). In its by-laws, the UUA stated that it would "cherish and spread the universal truths taught by the great prophets and teachers of humanity, immemorially summarized in the Judeo-Christian heritage as love to God and love to humanity." The Universalists wanted to say "<u>our</u> Judeo-Christian heritage" but the Unitarians insisted on saying "<u>the</u> Judeo-Christian heritage" because many of the Unitarians wanted to disassociate themselves from this identity.

One of the leading spokesmen for the Unitarian-Universalist Association was Dr. George N. Marshall, a humanist minister who led the Church of the Larger Fellowship, a 2,600 member UUA church-by-mail, for 25 years. In 1966, Dr. Marshall wrote a book, <u>Challenge of a Liberal Faith</u>, one of the most widely read books on Unitarian Universalism, which states that "Unitarian Universalists were a generation ahead of other churches with a non-theistic theology which we have called <u>humanism</u>."

A sample survey in 1981 showed that only 30% of the UUA church members affirmed a belief in God. In 1984, the UUA General Assembly proposed a new statement of Principles that deleted the affirmation of "love to God" from the UUA by-laws. This was approved by a final vote in the UUA General Assembly in 1985. The UUA decided to become a "pluralistic" organization that included persons of all religious or philosophical beliefs. "Unitarian Christianity," which evolved out of the anti-trinitarian movement of the 16th century CE, has virtually disappeared.

However, another movement, which became known as "Deism," began in the 17th century and opposed the trinitarian doctrines of the Christian church. All Deists agree that Jesus was simply human. The name "Deist" comes from the Latin word "Deus" which means "God." All Deists believe in one God, so they are "unitarians" in the true sense of this name, unlike some persons who claim the name "Unitarian Universalist" but do not believe in God. In the next chapter, we will examine the history of deism.

HISTORY OF DEISM

In the 17th century, CE (Christian Era or Common Era), in England, some ministers and others began to openly oppose church doctrines that appeared to be unfair or unreasonable. These individuals, who were called "Deists," were opposed to doctrines in the Church of England such as "original sin" which claims that human nature is inherently corrupt or evil because of the "original sin" (disobedience to God) by "Adam," the so-called "first man" according to the story in the book of Genesis in the Hebrew Bible.

The doctrine of "original sin" provided the foundation for the entire structure of trinitarian theology which was adopted by the church after several centuries. According to trinitarian theology, the corruption of human nature leads all persons to sin (disobey God) which is punishable by death in "hell," a place of everlasting torment. The trinitarian church claimed that human beings can only be "saved" from this punishment by believing that God's divine "Son" became a human being, Jesus, whose death was a "sacrificial atonement" to pay the "death penalty" as a "substitute" for humankind.

The deists rejected the church doctrine that belief in Jesus death is a prerequisite for forgiveness of sin because most human beings have never heard of Jesus during the history of the world. Deists believe that God would never treat people so unequally and unfairly.

With the claim to holding the only "keys to heaven and hell," the Christian church exerted tremendous influence after Christianity became an institutional religion officially recognized by the Roman Empire in the 4th century CE.

In the 5th century CE, the Roman Empire began to crumble. Germanic tribes (barbarians) invaded from the north and conquered Rome. The Roman emperor in Constantinople abandoned the western part of the empire (Italy, France, etc,). The Christian church filled the leadership vacuum in the west as Christian clergy performed civil administrative duties in addition to church duties.

Beginning in the 6th century (about 500 CE), Europe entered a period known as the "dark ages." Life for most people was depressing and tenuous because of poverty, disease, and war. The promise of a better life in the "hereafter" had great appeal, and the threat of "hell" for those who refused the offer of "salvation" gave the Christian church power over people, including government leaders. "Excommunication" meant that a person was excluded from church membership and thereby sentenced to "hell." With its growing power, the church gained wealth, especially in land.

Beginning about 1300 CE, the Renaissance came. There was renewed interest in the culture of the ancient Romans and Greeks, including literature, law, architecture, philosophy, and art. Interest in what the ancient Roman and Greek writers said in their original texts led to the development of textual criticism which could be applied to the Bible. Questions began to be raised about the text of the Vulgate (Latin) Bible used by the Roman Catholic Church.

The literature of ancient Rome and Greece offered a positive view of human nature and human potential. It did not have the negative and depressing view of human nature which is found in the church doctrine of "original sin." Roman and Greek culture emphasized the good and beauty in the world, and the responsibility of individuals for their own behavior.

Trade with the Far East (China and Japan) led to the discovery of cultures that existed continuously from before the time of "Noah" when the Bible claimed that the world had been destroyed by a flood. This raised questions about the reliability of the Bible.

Discovery and exploration of the "New World" (America) brought new wealth to European countries. Scientific discoveries in astronomy discredited the belief that the earth was the center of the universe as taught by the church. The invention of Gutenberg's printing press, about 1450, enabled the printing of thousands of religious tracts in the 1500's and later.

The Protestant Reformation began in the 1500's, leading to the development of Lutheran and Reformed (Calvinist) churches. The Protestant reformers opposed the authority of the Roman Catholic pope but made no effort to reform trinitarian theology.

The Renaissance and the Protestant Reformation brought religious, philosophical, and political changes in Europe and England. The 1600's brought scientific advances in medicine, chemistry, physics, and astronomy. Isaac Newton's theories about the universe and gravity presented new ways of looking at the world.

In the latter half of the 1600's (the seventeenth century), a number of Anglican ministers and other writers began to question trinitarian doctrines that appeared to be contrary to nature and reason. These writings continued through the 1700's, and the name "deism" was given to the views expressed by these writers.

Deism was not an organized religious movement in England. It was an effort by individuals to reform Christian theology by challenging church doctrines that were inconsistent with the teachings of Jesus and human reason.

Deists opposed the doctrines of original sin, divinity of Jesus, substitutionary atonement through the death of Jesus, and punishment of non-Christians by torture in "hell." Deists also rejected the Calvinist doctrine of "predestination" that claimed that individuals were either "saved" or "lost" (condemned to "hell") before they were born. This doctrine made God appear to be a cruel and arbitrary tyrant. Deists also rejected the concept of "supernatural revelation" of truth, and belief in "miracles" contrary to nature.

In contrast to trinitarian doctrines, English deists wrote that (1) the existence of a Creator (God) is inferred by human reasoning from purposeful design found in nature, (2) individuals should worship (honor) God by virtuous behavior (love for others), (3) individuals are accountable for their behavior, and (4) repentance is the means for obtaining God's forgiveness for wrong- doing.

The writings of the English Deists occurred mostly in the 1600's and 1700's. Edward Herbert (1581-1648) was an early proponent of natural and universal religion based on human reason. Although Herbert did not claim to be a "deist," some of his ideas were adopted later by deists, so Herbert is sometimes called the "Father of Deism." Charles Blount (1654-1693) was the first identifiable deist in England. Blount wrote a book <u>Religio Laici</u>("Layman's Religion") in 1683, based on Edward Herbert's book De Religione Laici ("A Layman's Religion") which was published in 1645.

Blount also published a book, entitled *Oracles of Reason* in 1693, containing an article "A Summary Account of the Deists Religion," the earliest published statement of deist beliefs.

Blount rejected the doctrines of the "Trinity of God" and substitutionary atonement through the death of Jesus.

Blount questioned the stories of "miracles" in the Bible, and he believed that much of traditional Christianity had been invented by priests and other religious leaders.

The English philosopher John Locke (1632-1704) was not a deist but he wrote a book *On the Reasonableness of Christianity* in 1695. Locke viewed Jesus as the "messiah" or "Son of God" sent to confirm the truths that could be known through human reasoning. Locke did not deny the idea of "supernatural revelation" of truth but he believed that any alleged revelation had to b e reasonable. Locke was willing to accept some church doctrines that were "mysteries," or beyond human comprehension, if such doctrines were not contrary to reason. Locke considered himself an Anglican Christian but he admitted that human reason could discover the same truths that were taught by Jesus. Locke wrote his book, *On the Reasonableness of Christianity*, in an effort to support what he considered to be "orthodox" Christianity, in opposition to deism, but his book unintentionally gave support to deist beliefs, and led trinitarian clergy to accuse Locke of being an anti-trinitarian.

John Toland (1670-1722) published a book *Christianity Not Mysterious*, in 1696 (one year after Locke's book mentioned above), in which Toland wrote that any doctrine that was "mysterious," or beyond human comprehension, was not essential to Christianity. Toland believed that God would not expect anyone to believe something that was beyond human comprehension or was contrary to reason. The trinitarian clergy recognized that Toland was questioning the doctrine of the "Trinity of God." Toland's book was burned in Ireland, and the Church of England brought charges against Toland.

Thomas Woolston (1669-1733) was an Anglican minister who believed that the events recorded in the "Old" and

New Testaments should not be taken literally and historically, but had to be interpreted allegorically. These included stories about the virgin birth and miracles of Jesus. Woolston was imprisoned for "blasphemy" which was considered a religious and civil offense.

Matthew Tindal (165?-1733) was an Anglican lawyer and writer who wrote *Christianity as Old as Creation, or the Gospel, a Republication of the Religion of Nature* in 1730. Tindal believed that God's revelation came through nature as understood through human reasoning. Tindal rejected the doctrine of "original sin." Tindal believed that God's truth cannot be limited to a particular place or time, as it is as old as creation.

Thomas Morgan (169?-1743) was ordained as a Presbyterian minister in 1717 and later became a medical doctor. He wrote a book *The Moral Philosopher*, in 1737, in which he identified himself as a "Christian Deist." Morgan agreed with Matthew Tindal that Christianity is essentially a republication of truths found in "natural religion" which is known as "deism." Henry St. John (1672-1751), also known as Viscount Bolingbroke, was a prominent politician who served as Secretary of State and Secretary of War at various times in the government of England. When his political party was out of power, St. John began studying philosophy and became a deist in his religious philosophy. He was personally acquainted with the French philosopher Voltaire who had a high regard for St. John as a philosopher. St. John was also acquainted with the poet Alexander Pope whose poetry was influenced by St. John's deism. St. John's belief in the existence of God was based on design in nature. He wrote, "When we contemplate the works of God . . . they give us very clear and determined ideas of wisdom and power, which we call infinite . . ."

Thomas Chubb (1679-1747) was a humble candle-maker

and brilliant writer. His writings brought him to the attention of some Unitarians with whom he associated in London for a few years but he returned home to his life as a candle-maker and writer. In 1739, he published *The True Gospel of Jesus Christ Asserted*. Chubb considered himself to be a Christian Deist, and his writings brought deism to ordinary people.

Peter Annet (1693-1769) was a school master and prolific writer. In *Deism Fairly Stated*, in 1744, Annet wrote that "Deism . . . is not other than the Religion essential to Man, the original religion of Reason and Nature, such as was believed and practiced by Socrates, and others of old . . ." Annet questioned the validity of miracles and held a very low opinion of the "apostle Paul." Annet also questioned the records of the "resurrection" of Jesus.

Annet was the editor/publisher of a periodical called <u>Free Enquirer</u> in which he questioned Old Testament history. For this, Annet was imprisoned for one month and had to stand in pillory. Later, in his sixties, Annet was arrested again for "blasphemous libel" and was sentenced to one year of hard labor in prison. After his release, Annet returned to school teaching in a grammar school until his death.

Religious and political conditions in England prepared the way for the development of deism in the 17th century. Anglican ministers and university professors were familiar with rationalism since the days of Robert Hooker (1554-1600), an Anglican theologian. The English revolution of 1688 brought changes in civil government, and eventually some freedom of the press. The Protestant Reformation gave rise to various Christian denominations in England.

But the Protestant Reformation was not aimed at reforming trinitarian theology. The early deists undertook this task by rejecting the doctrines that had been developed after the time of Jesus. Deists saw themselves as carrying the Protestant Reformation to its logical conclusion by trying to reform Christian theology. Deists summarized Christianity as belief in God and love for each other, as taught by Jesus and known through nature, experience, and human reasoning.

In England, deism existed primarily in the writings of individuals who expressed their personal religious beliefs. Occasionally, there were private meetings of small groups for discussion.

In France, during the French Revolution, an effort was made to replace the Roman Catholic Church with a form of non-Christian deism. The Roman Catholic Church and the French monarchy were viewed as allies in suppressing the French people, so the church and monarchy were attacked simultaneously. During the revolution, the Notre Dame Cathedral in Paris was renamed "The Temple of Reason." But the effort to replace the Roman Catholic Church with the "Cult of the Supreme Being" did not succeed. Non-Christian deism was too abstract to attract the general population. In 1797, Thomas Paine tried to organize a non- Christian deist group called the "Society of Theophilanthropists" in Paris. The name meant "lovers of God and mankind," but the group did not survive.

In the United States, English deism did have some influence in the late 18th and early 19th centuries. English philosophy and religion came to the United States through books and personal communications between individuals in both countries.

Ethan Allen (1737-1788), a hero of the American Revolution, was the first well-known deist in America when it was under British rule. In 1756, Allen moved to Salisbury, Connecticut, where he became a deist during his acquaintance with Dr. Thomas Young, a physician and deist, who lived just north of Salisbury, in the New York colony. Allen and Young began writing a book on deism but Young moved to Albany, New York, in 1764, and took the manuscript with him. In 1781, Allen acquired the manuscript from Dr. Young's widow, and Allen completed the book entitled *Reason the Only Oracle of Man, or a Compendious System of Natural Religion* in 1782. The book was not published until 1784 because Allen had difficulty finding money to pay a printer. Since Allen wrote that he had never read any writings by a deist, the English deism in the book apparently came from Dr. Thomas Young.

Dr. Thomas Young (1731-1777) was a prominent physician who practiced medicine in western New York, in Boston, Massachusetts, and in Philadelphia, Pennsylvania. Young was a patriot in the American independence movement, and a leader in the "Boston Tea Party," one of the events that led to the start of the American Revolution.

Dr. Young was a frequent writer of medical and political articles in newspapers and a magazine. His religious views were well-known, and his deistic creed was stated in a letter published in a newspaper, the Massachusetts Spy, in 1772. This is the earliest published creed by a deist in America. Also, Young was apparently the primary author of the manuscript on which Ethan Allen based his book, *Reason the Only Oracle of Man*, published in 1784 after Dr. Young's death.

Dr. Young wrote that his religion was based on two principles:
> "1st. To believe that God is, and is the rewarder of all those that diligently seek him.
> 2nd. To do justly, and to love mercy among us being, As ye would that others do unto you do also unto them in like manner."

Young's statement is a concise summary of deism. Believe that God exists and rewards those who sincerely seek "to do justly and love mercy" (Micah 6:8), which means "whatever (good) you wish that other people would do to you, do so unto them" (Matthew 7:12).

Young wrote, "I believe that in the order of nature and providence, the man who most assiduously endeavors to promote the will of God in the good of their fellow creatures, receives the simple reward of his virtue, the peace of mind and silent applause of a good conscience, which administers more solid satisfaction than all of the other enjoyments of life put together."

Thomas Paine (1737-1809) emigrated from England to America in 1774, and became famous for his writings which inspired Americans to seek independence from England. Paine was active in the American Revolutionary War, and his writings were credited by George Washington for rallying financial and moral support for the American army when it appeared that America was losing the war for independence. Paine wrote his deistic book, *The Age of Reason*, in 1794, opposing both trinitarian Christianity and atheism. Paine would not call himself a "Christian" because he equated "Christianity" with the "trinitarian" doctrines of the church.

Thomas Jefferson (1743-1826) was clearly a deist. When Jefferson wrote the Declaration of Independence, he referred to "the laws of nature and nature's God." Although he was reared in the Episcopal Church and participated in the parish, Jefferson held deistic views. In a letter to John Adams, Jefferson wrote, "I hold (without appeal to revelation) that when we take a view of the Universe, in its parts, general and particular, it is impossible for the human mind not to perceive and feel a conviction of design, of consummate skill, indefinite power in every atom of composition . . . it is impossible, I say, for the human mind not to believe that there is . . . a fabricator of all things."

Jefferson believed that the teachings of Jesus had "been disfigured by the corruptions of schismatizing followers" but Jefferson believed that Jesus taught "the most sublime and benevolent code of morals which has ever been offered to man." Jefferson made his own "Bible" by extracting what he found to be valid in the life and teachings of Jesus. This "cut and paste" version is now called "The Jefferson Bible." It omits the "miracles" of Jesus and makes no mention of the "resurrection" of Jesus.

To Jefferson, religion is a private matter. He wrote, "I have ever thought religion a concern purely between God and our consciences for which we are accountable to him, and not to priests."

Elihu Palmer (1764-1806), an ex-Presbyterian minister, was a deist who was active in preaching deism and organizing Deistical Societies in New York and Pennsylvania. He also edited and published deistic newspapers. Palmer rejected his previous identity as a Presbyterian minister and he viewed Christianity as superstition. In 1801, Palmer wrote <u>The Principles of Nature</u>, as follows:

"1. The universe proclaims the existence of one supreme Deity, worthy of the adoration of intelligent beings.

2. Man is possessed of moral and intellectual facilities sufficient for the improvement of nature, and for the acquisition of happiness.

3. The religion of nature is the only religion, it grows out of the moral relations of intelligent beings, and it is connected with the progressive improvement and common welfare of

the human race.

4. It is essential to the true interest of man, that he love truth and practice virtue.

5. Vice is everywhere ruinous and destructive to the happiness of the individual and society. A benevolent disposition, and beneficent actions, are the fundamental duties of rational beings.

6. A religion mingled with persecution and malice cannot be of divine origin.

7. Education and science are essential to the happiness of man.

8. Civil and religious liberty is essential to his interests.

9. There can be no human authority to which man ought to be answerable for his religious opinions.

10. Science and truth, virtue and happiness, are the great objects to which the activity and energy of human faculties ought to be directed."

Benjamin Franklin (1706-1790) was reared in the Calvinism of the Presbyterian Church but as a youth working in his brother's print shop, Franklin saw some anti-deist literature which had the opposite effect on Franklin. Franklin said that he then became a "thorough deist" but, at age 19, he briefly adopted a materialistic philosophy. He then returned to the Presbyterian Church, in Philadelphia, but he ceased attending it when he was 22 years of age. Franklin wrote his own "Articles of Belief and Acts of Religion" for his own use.

Franklin kept his personal religious beliefs very private but in old age he wrote: "I believe in one God, Creator of the

Universe. That he governs it by Providence. That he ought to be worshipped. That the most acceptable Service we render him is doing good to his other Children. That the soul of man is immortal, and will be treated with justice in another Life respecting its Conduct in this. These I take to be the fundamental Principles of all sound Religion "

Franklin deism can be seen in his statements, "I believe in one God, Creator of the Universe" and "The most acceptable Service to him is doing good to his other Children." However, Franklin appears to presume that each human soul is immortal and "will be treated with justice in another Life respecting its conduct in this." Franklin presumption that each human soul is immortal and has "another Life" after this present life is not a principle of deism. Deists would agree that God has the power to give another life to an individual after "this" life but not for the purpose of rendering "justice" (reward and punishment) in "another Life" with respect to the individual's "conduct in this" life, as Benjamin Franklin asserted.

Matthew Tindal, a deist who wrote *Christianity as Old as Creation*, in 1730, believed that God would not punish a person except to reform him/her. Tindal wrote, "It was for the sake of Man that He (God) gave him Laws, so He (God) executes them purely for the same reason, since upon His (God's) account, He can't the least bit affected, whether His laws be, or not be observed; and consequently in punishing, no more than in rewarding, does He (God) act as a Party, much less an injured Party, who wants Satisfaction, or Reparation of Honour. And indeed, to suppose it, is highly to dishonor Him, since God, as He can never be injured, so He can never want Reparation." Tindal continues, "All Punishment for Punishment's sake is meer Cruelty and Malice, which can never be in God; nor can He hate anything He has made, or be subject to such Weakness or Impotence as to act arbitrarily, or out of Spite, Wrath, Revenge, or any Self-Interest; and consequently, whatever Punishment He (God) inflicts, must be a Mark of His Love, in not suffering (allowing) his Creatures to remain in that miserable State, which is inseparable from Sin and Wickedness." Tindal wrote, "because God, whose love infinitely exceeds that of mortal parents, chastises his Children (and all mankind are alike his Offspring) because He loves them and designs (desires) their Amendment (correction)." Tindal adds, "As God's infinite Goodness appears in the sanctions a well as the Matter of His Laws, so His infinite Wisdom knows how to adjust the Punishment to the Offense; that it may be exactly fitted to produce the desired Amendment."

Tindal rejected the church doctrine that Jesus' death on the cross was required to satisfy God's "wrath" or make "Reparation" to God, and "to suppose it is to highly dishonor Him (God)." Tindal rejected "Punishment for punishment's sake" as "mere Cruelty and Malice, which can never be in God." Tindal believed that any punishment is intended "to produce Amendment" (correction) in human beings so they would not "remain in that miserable State, which is inseparable from Sin and Wickedness."

The deist Thomas Young wrote, "The man who most assiduously endeavors to promote the will of God in the good of his fellow creatures receives the most simple reward of his virtue, the peace of mind and silent applause of a good conscience, which renders more solid satisfaction than all the other enjoyments of life put together." Young believed that the reward to an individual for good behavior toward "fellow creatures" comes now in "peace of mind," approval from "a good conscience," and "solid satisfaction" with oneself. What Thomas Young believed can be verified by our own experience.

Deists agree with Matthew Tindal and Thomas Young that normal human beings are affected by their own behavior.

A person's "sin and wickedness" is punished by a "miserable State" (of self-dissatisfaction) within a normal person. "Endeavors to promote the will of God in the good of his fellow creatures" are rewarded by "peace of mind and silent applause of good conscience" in self-satisfaction.

Ralph Waldo Emerson (1803-1882), a Unitarian minister and philosopher, expressed a similar view. Emerson wrote, "In the soul of man there is a justice whose retributions are instant and entire. He who does a good deed, is instantly enobled. He who does a mean deed, is by the action itself contracted. Its operation in life, though slow to the senses, is, at last, sure in the soul. By it, a man is made the Providence to himself, dispensing good to his goodness, and evil to his sin . . . Benevolence is absolute and real. So much benevolence as a man hath, so much life hath he. While a man seeks good ends, he is strong by the whole strength of nature. In so far as he roves from these ends, he bereaves himself of power, of auxiliaries; his being shrinks out of all remote channels, he becomes less and less, a mote, a point, until absolute badness is absolute death."

In Emerson's view, justice is experienced instantly within a person. By good deeds, life in the soul is "enobled" (increased), and by bad deeds, life in the soul is "contracted" (reduced). Emerson believed that "absolute" badness brings "absolute death" to the soul. Ethan Allen published his (and Dr. Thomas Young's) book, *Reason the Only Oracle of Man*, in 1784, only after Young's death (in 1777) and shortly before Allen's death (in 1788), but this book had little or no immediate influence on the deist movement in the United States.

Thomas Jefferson and Benjamin Franklin kept their deism very private because both were prominent political leaders and they wanted to avoid controversy over religion.

Thomas Paine and Elihu Palmer were active in trying to organize the deist movement, but both made the mistake of equating "Christianity" and "trinitarianism." Both Paine and Palmer exposed the irrationality of trinitarian theology, but they showed no acquaintance with the English deists who respected the human Jesus as a teacher of natural and universal religion. With the deaths of Palmer (in 1806) and Paine (in 1809), most deist publications ceased, and efforts to organize a deist movement ended in the United States.

In recent years, there has been a revival of interest in deism. The internet has provided more communication between individuals who are interested in natural religion based on human observation, experience, and reasoning. Individuals are experimenting with ways to bring deists together for mutual support and promotion of deism. I believe that the teachings of Jesus make the principles of deism understandable and provide a personal religion that can be practiced every day. I am a deist, and I believe that Jesus was a great teacher of deism. This is why I call myself a "Christian Deist."

In the next chapter, we will examine the principles of deism in the teachings of Jesus.

DEISM IN THE TEACHINGS OF JESUS

Since life comes to you through no decision of your own, this is evidence that life comes from a Source beyond yourself. From the intricate and purposeful designs seen in nature (the world and human life), Deists infer that human life originated intentionally, not accidentally. The intentional Originator is usually called "God" (the Latin word for "God" is "deus" from which "deists" receive their name). Deists do not presume to describe God but they believe that God is what gives life to human beings.

Each person is faced with the question, "How shall I live the life that I have received?" Deists believe that the answer to this question is found in the design of human nature. From observation, experience, and reasoning, Deists recognize that human beings are designed to be interdependent creatures. We are dependent on each other for survival and for satisfaction in living. As infants, we are totally dependent on others for survival. Gradually, as we grow up, we take more responsibility for our own care and for giving care to others.

From the design of human nature, it is natural for a human being to love (value) his or her own self. This "self-love" is the means for evaluating human behavior. If another person's action is hurtful or uncaring to you, you instinctively know that this action is "wrong." Using your power of reason (logical thinking), you can recognize that your own actions that are hurtful or uncaring toward other persons are also "wrong." The ability to evaluate one's own behavior (sometimes called "conscience") enables human beings to usually avoid doing "wrong," or to recognize when they have done "wrong." In a mentally normal person, the ability to evaluate one's own behavior increases as that person matures and learns from his or her observations and experiences.

Wrong behavior violates the design of human nature, and is disturbing to the violator to the extent of his or her ability to know right and wrong. Wrong behavior causes self-condemnation (guilt) and loss of self-respect within a person of normal mentality and sufficient age (maturity).

In religious terms, wrong behavior is called "sin." Relief from the psychological misery caused by guilt can come from repentance by the violator (wrong-doer). Repentance is a process in which the violator recognizes his or her wrong behavior, feels remorse over it, stops the wrong behavior, and seeks to make amends for the wrong, if possible. Repentance of wrong behavior enables a person to feel relief from the guilt, and to regain self-respect and peace of mind.

Deism is based on the premise that God designed us to care for each other. A Jewish rabbi named Jesus expressed this as "You shall love your neighbor as (you love) yourself" (Matthew 22:39). As explained above, it is natural for a person to love oneself, and this "self-love" enables a person to know what it means to love others, as expressed by Jesus, "Whatever (good) you wish that others would do to you, do so unto them" (Matthew 7:12). This natural law has become known as the "Golden Rule" for how we ought to care for each other. This truth is validated through our own observation, experience, and reasoning. Deism is essentially the natural religion of the Golden Rule. Deists who recognize the principles of deism in the teachings of Jesus are known as "Christian Deists." The name "Christian" comes from the Greek word "christos" which means "anointed." The earliest followers of Jesus were called "Christians" because they believed that Jesus was "anointed" (chosen) to establish the "Kingdom of God" on earth. Today, the name "Christian" is used as a general term by all persons who claim to be followers of Jesus regardless of their differences in beliefs about him.

Christian Deists believe that Jesus was simply a human being who understood and taught the way that God intends for people to live. Jesus described himself as "a man who told you the truth which I heard from God" (John 8:40) but Jesus did not make any exclusive claim to learning from God. Jesus said, "It is written in the prophets (Isaiah 54:13), 'And they shall all be taught by God" (John 6:45). Christian Deists believe that people are taught by God through the power of reasoning that God has given to them, and from their own observations and experiences.

Let us now examine the basic teachings of Jesus in which the principles of Christian Deism are found:

FIRST, Jesus taught GOD GIVES LIFE TO HUMAN BEINGS. Jesus said, "God is spirit" (John 4:24) and "it is the spirit that gives life" (John 6:63) (Also, Luke 23:46). It is obvious to an individual human being that life comes to that person through no decision of his or her own. From this, Christian Deists infer the existence of a life-giver which Deists call "God."

As a Jew, Jesus expressed his belief in God as stated in the Shema, the traditional Jewish affirmation of belief in God. The Hebrew word "shema" means "hear" which is the first word in the Shema, "Hear, O Israel: The Lord our God, the Lord is one; and you shall love the Lord your God with all your heart, and with all your soul, and with all your might." The Shema is found in the Hebrew scriptures (Deuteronomy 6:4). The authors of the books of Matthew and Mark give slightly different wording but it is clear that Jesus is referring to the Hebrew Shema (Matthew 22:34-38; Mark 12:28-30) when Jesus expressed his belief in God.

Jesus taught that we show our love (appreciation) to God by how we use the life that has been entrusted to us.

Jesus illustrated this truth in his parable of the Talents (Matthew 25:14-30). In this story, an employer entrusted three of his servants with various amounts of money (called "talents") to invest for the employer. Two of the servants did as they were instructed, so the employer entrusted them with more money to manage in the future. Another servant showed disrespect for the employer by refusing to invest the money which that servant had received, so the employer took back the money and the unfaithful servant lost his employment.

The parable of the "Talents" could be called the parable of "Life." God gives us varying amounts of time, abilities, and opportunities to invest in this world. How we choose to live in this world shows our respect or lack of respect for God who entrusted life to us.

SECOND, Jesus taught YOU SHALL LOVE YOUR NEIGHBOR AS YOURSELF (Matthew 22:39). This means you shall love your neighbor as you love yourself. It is natural for a person to love (care about) his or her own self, and this self-love shows us what it means to love (care about) other persons. Jesus said, "Whatever (good) you wish that others would do to you, do so unto them (Matthew 7:12). This has become known as the "Golden Rule." This natural law is intended to govern the behavior of all human beings.

When Jesus said, "You shall love your neighbor as yourself," it is important to know Jesus' definition of "neighbor." As a Jew, Jesus had been taught to "love your neighbor as yourself" as stated in the book of Leviticus in the Hebrew Bible. Leviticus 19:18 states, "you shall not take vengeance or bear a grudge against the sons of your own people but you shall love your neighbor as yourself." Here, "neighbor" is defined as "sons of your own people" or, in other words, your Hebrew (Jewish) neighbors. The only exception to this definition is made in Leviticus 19:33-34, "When a stranger sojourns with you in your land, you shall do him no wrong. The stranger who sojourns with you shall be <u>as a native</u> among you, and you shall love him as yourself, for you (the Jews) were strangers in the land of Egypt . . ."

The book of Leviticus defines "neighbor" as "sons of your own people" (Leviticus 19:18) and "strangers who sojourn with you in your land" (Leviticus 19:33). In other words, "neighbor" only included persons who were Jews, or other persons who were allowed to live in the Jews' country. There was no requirement that the Jews love anyone else, and this was clearly demonstrated when Moses ordered the Hebrew army to kill people who were considered "enemies" as the Hebrews marched through other countries on the way to invade the land of Canaan (Deuteronomy 20:10-17).

Jesus defined "neighbor" to include everyone, even "enemies." Jesus said, "You have heard it said, 'You shall love your neighbor and hate your enemy.' But I say to you, Love your enemies and pray for those who persecute you, so that you may be sons of your Father who is in heaven; for He (God) makes the sun rise on the evil and the good, and sends rain on the just and the unjust" (Matthew 5:43-45).

Of course, sunshine and rain are required to produce food needed by all human beings, the evil and good, the just and the unjust. We should follow God's example in caring about the needs of all people. Deism is the religion of the Golden Rule, "Do good to others as you would have others do good to you." The wisdom of the Golden Rule is recognized by persons who profess various religions and by persons who profess no religion. This natural law is the essential guide for human survival and satisfaction in living.

The Golden Rule is validated by human observation, experience, and reasoning. By doing good to others, normal persons reward themselves with a feeling of self-approval (happiness). By failing to do good to others, normal persons punish themselves with a feeling of self-disapproval (unhappiness).

THIRD, Jesus taught that FAILURE TO LOVE OTHERS IS WRONG. The failure to love others occurs when (1) we intentionally cause human suffering, or (2) we are indifferent to human suffering. Being hurtful or uncaring toward others is called "sin." Jesus illustrated this truth in his parable of the Good Samaritan (Luke 10:30-37). In this story, robbers caused human suffering by beating and robbing a Jewish traveler. Two other persons were indifferent to the suffering of the Jew, and passed by without trying to help the man. Finally, a Samaritan came to the rescue of the beaten Jew and took care of him. At the time when Jesus told this parable, the Jews and Samaritans were considered "enemies" to each other so this story illustrated what it means to love (care about) everyone, even those who are considered "enemies."

<u>FOURTH</u>, Jesus taught that SIN IS FORGIVEN IF A PERSON REPENTS OF THE WRONG-DOING.

Jesus illustrated this truth in his parable of the "Prodigal Son" (Luke 15:11-24). In this story, a young man asked his father for money which the son squandered in "loose living." When the son realized that he had done wrong, the son was remorseful. The son confessed his "sin" to his father, and offered to make amends by working as a "hired servant" for the father. The father forgave the son and welcomed him back into the family. In this story, Jesus taught that repentance includes remorse for wrong behavior, stopping the behavior, confessing the wrong, and willingness to make amends for the wrong.

According to Jesus, God forgives our sins (failures to love) if we repent and we are willing to forgive others who repent of their sins against us. Jesus said, "If you forgive men their trespasses, your heavenly Father will also forgive you but if you do not forgive men their trespasses (against you), neither will your Father forgive your trespasses" (Matthew 6:14-15). Jesus said, "If your brother sins, rebuke him, and if he repents, forgive him; and if he turns to you seven times, and says, 'I repent, you must forgive him (Luke 17:3-4).

Christian Deists reject the idea, taught by trinitarian Christians, that God requires that a "death penalty" for sins be paid (by Jesus' death) before God will forgive the sins of human beings. Jesus plainly taught that God will "forgive us our sins as we forgive those who sin against us" (Matthew 6:12) and that repentance is the only prerequisite for receiving forgiveness (Luke 17:3-4).

FIFTH, Jesus taught that GOD'S KINGDOM COMES ON EARTH AS GOD'S WILL IS DONE
(Matthew 6:10), and God's will is "You shall love your neighbor as yourself" (Mark 12:31). Christian Deists believe that we worship (honor) God by using our time, abilities, and opportunities in doing God's will to help make this world a better place for each other. Jesus taught that the "kingdom of God" exists wherever the will of God is done by individuals and in society.

Christian Deists do not have places for public worship (such as churches, temples, mosques). Jesus said, "When you pray, you must not be like the hypocrites; for they love to stand in the synagogues and at the street corners, that they may be seen by men . . . But when you pray, go into your room and shut the door and pray to your Father who is in secret; and your Father who sees in secret will reward you" (Matthew 6:5-6). Jesus also said, "When you give alms, do not let your left hand know what your right hand is doing, so that your alms may be in secret; and your Father who sees in secret will reward you (Matthew 6:3-4). Christian Deists believe that prayer and charitable giving should be done privately. Christian Deists worship (honor) God by doing God's will in loving (caring about) other persons. This can be done wherever we are.

<u>SIXTH</u>, Jesus taught that THE LIFE-GIVING SPIRIT IN A HUMAN BEING RETURNS TO GOD
at the time of physical death. When Jesus thought that he was dying, he prayed to God, "Into Thy hands, I commit my spirit" (Luke 23:46). Christian Deists do not presume to know what the future will bring after this life, but we can face death with peace of mind. The life we have now is evidence that God has the power to give life, so it is reasonable to believe that God is able to give us another life if this is God's will. If we sincerely try to live now by love for each other, and we repent of our failures to love, we have done all that we can do, and we can trust our future in God's care, as Jesus trusted in God. Christian Deists have reason to live with hope.

In the next chapter, we will examine how a person can practice Christian Deism as a personal religion.

PRACTICE OF CHRISTIAN DEISM

Your personal religion consists of the beliefs that you live by. A "belief" is a proposition that you think is true. If your behavior (words and actions) is guided by a particular belief, then this is a "belief that you live by." If a particular belief is only a proposition that does not actually influence your behavior, such a belief is not part of your personal religion.

Deism is based on the the fact that life comes to each of us through no decision or action of our own. In using the word "life," I am referring to the individual "self" or personal consciousness that you find within your physical body. This is sometimes called "soul" or "spirit" or "being." A man named Jesus used the term "spirit." He said, "It is the spirit that gives life . . ." (John 6:63).

Deists believe that a Creator (usually called "God") intentionally created the world and humankind. Deists do not presume to describe God but infer the existence of God from the intricate and purposeful designs observed in nature -- both in the world and humankind. Scientists have discovered "design" in the universe, such as the orbiting of the Earth around the sun at a distance that enables life to exist on Earth. Scientists have also discovered "design" in the human body and its functioning.

Deists believe that human beings are designed to live by love for each other. Any failure to love (care about) another person is a violation of human nature and is destructive to the spirit within the violator. It is a failure to love if a person (1) causes human suffering, or (2) is indifferent to human suffering. A failure to love is called "sin" because it is an offense to God and humankind.

Jesus expressed the essence of deism in terms that came from his Jewish culture. When Jesus was asked, "Which is the first (greatest) commandment of God?" Jesus referred to the Jewish "Shema." Shema is the Hebrew word for "hear." It is the first word in the traditional Jewish affirmation of respect for God, "Hear, O Israel, the Lord our God is one Lord, and you shall love the Lord your God with all your heart, and with all your soul, and with all your might" (Deuteronomy 6:4). Jesus said, "This is the great and first commandment. And the second is like it, You shall love your neighbor as yourself. On these two commandments depend all of the law (of God) and (the teachings) of the prophets" (Matthew 22:34-40). It is significant that Jesus said that "love your neighbor as yourself" is _like_ "love the Lord your God." Christian Deists believe that we show our love for God by loving our neighbor as ourselves. These are two sides of the same coin.

Christian Deists see the premise and principles of deism in these teachings of Jesus. The Shema begins with the premise of deism, an affirmation that God exists ("The Lord our God is one.")

Then the first principle of deism is stated as "You shall love God with all your heart, with all your soul, and with all your might." This means loving God with your whole person: (1) heart (mind or will), (2) soul (inner self or being), and (3) might (physical body or strength). We should show respect for God by our thoughts and words, by our integrity, and by our actions. Deists worship (show respect for) God by living as God designed us to live.

The second principle of deism is stated as "You shall love your neighbor as yourself." It is important to note that "love your neighbor" is related to "as yourself." The requirement to "love your neighbor" is based on the assumption that you love _yourself_. In other words, you must first recognize the value of your own life, or have self-respect, before you can fully appreciate the value of your neighbor's life.

When Jesus was asked, "Who is my neighbor?" he answered with the parable of the "Good Samaritan." In this parable, Jesus defined "neighbor" as EVERYONE, even persons who are considered to be "enemies." (As explained in Chapter Four above.)

Jesus said, "You have heard it said, 'You shall love your neighbor but hate your enemy.' But I say to you, Love your enemy and pray for those who persecute you, so that you may be sons of your Father (God) who is in heaven; for He makes his sun rise on the evil and on the good, and sends his rain on the just and on the unjust" (Matthew 5:43-45.)

What did Jesus mean by "love your enemies?" We may resist this idea because our enemies are usually persons who have offended us or threatened us in some way. Jesus did not mean that we should be passive toward someone who seriously threatens our lives. On the night that Jesus was arrested, he and his disciples obviously felt that their lives were in danger because Peter said, "Lord (sir), I am ready to go with you to prison or death" (Luke 22:33.) Then Jesus urged his disciples to arm themselves with knives (Luke 22:36). Jesus apparently believed in the right of self-defense. But, later when one of the disciples made a "first strike" with his knife, Jesus condemned the action, saying, "No more of this" (Luke 22:50-51).

So what did Jesus mean by "love your enemies?" Jesus said, "Love your enemies and do good . . . for He (God) is kind to the ungrateful and selfish. Be merciful, even as your Father (God) is merciful" (Luke 6:35-36). These are the key words, "merciful," "kind, and "do good" to those who hate you, or are unlikeable (e.g, "ungrateful" or "selfish")." Loving" your enemy does not mean that you approve of hateful, ungrateful, or selfish behavior. It means "be merciful" or compassionate toward anyone who suffers, even your enemies or people whom you do not like.

Today, in our world, we can see how fear and hatred can lead people to see others as "enemies" who must be destroyed. The hatred expressed in the cycle of revenge -- an eye for and eye -- has blinded people from recognizing that their "enemies" are often persons who are suffering from poverty, disease, exploitation, and hopelessness. They need help. What would happen if someone tried to be "merciful" and "do good" to them. To relieve suffering could turn an enemy into a friend.

What would happen if we sat down with our "enemies" to find out what they need from us, and to tell them what we need from them? Maybe we could find some ways to help each other, and achieve a better world for all of us -- a world that Jesus called "the kingdom of God" on earth.

The everyday practice of Christian Deism means following the natural way of love, or compassion, for all people. We show our appreciation to God for the gift of life in three ways:

(1) by respecting the value of our own life, (2) by respecting the value of life in other persons, and (3) by respecting the value of the natural resources of the Earth on which life depends.

<u>RESPECT THE VALUE OF ONE'S OWN LIFE BY:</u>

1. Taking care of your health. We should not neglect or abuse our physical body by abusing alcohol and other drugs, eating unhealthy food, eating too much or too little, failing to exercise and rest, or neglecting personal cleanliness.

2. Doing your share of work required to maintain human society. We should not neglect the care of our home or family. To the extent that we are able, we should support

ourselves and contribute to the economy of the
community.

3.   Enjoying your life. A person can find much joy in
common things and everyday experiences. Enjoyment
does not depend on having wealth and expensive
pleasures.

RESPECT THE VALUE OF LIFE IN OTHER PERSONS BY:

1. Not being hurtful to other persons by causing them to
    suffer.

2.   Not being uncaring toward other persons by being
indifferent to their suffering.

3. Taking care of other persons, or helping them to take
care of themselves, as their situations require.

RESPECT THE VALUE OF THE NATURAL RESOURCES OF THE EARTH BY:

1. Using the natural resources of the Earth wisely,
renewing them, and by sharing them fairly with all other
persons.

2. Not damaging the land, water, and air by neglect,
    exploitation, or pollution.

3.   Avoiding overpopulation that depletes limited natural
resources of the Earth. The population of the Earth has
increased from 3 billion to 7 billion persons in the last 50
years. The uncontrolled growth of population is depleting
the natural resources of the Earth, and is the underlying
cause of mass starvation and most wars to obtain natural
resources. Population growth should be controlled

through family planning, sex education, contraceptives, and voluntary sterilization.

A CLOSING WORD

Deism is natural religion. Its principles can be known through human observation, experience, and reasoning. Deists who recognize that a man named Jesus taught this natural religion are known as "Christian Deists." True religion is not found in a book; it is found in ourselves. It is my hope that my little book will be helpful as you discover natural religion in yourself.

In my understanding of deism, two books were especially helpful to me. I have included excerpts from these two books in Appendix One and Appendix Two. The first book is *The Age of Reason* (parts one and two) (1794, 1795) by Thomas Paine. This book is available in many bookstores. I prefer the paperback Citadel Press Book published by the Carol Publishing Group, New York, NY, because it has an excellent Introduction by Philip S. Foner who includes a brief biography of Thomas Paine. The second book is *Christianity as Old as Creation: or, the Gospel, a Republication of the Religion of Nature* (1730) by Matthew Tindal. A photographic reproduction of Tindal's book has been printed by Routledge/Thommes Press, London, England, and can be purchased from some book stores via the internet.

Thomas Paine (1737-1809) was a deist but he did not consider himself a "Christian Deist" because the only Christianity that Paine knew was trinitarian Christianity. In fact, in his writings, Paine makes the mistake of using the term "Christianity" as defined by trinitarian churches when Paine rejects the doctrines of these churches. Readers of Paine's writings need to be aware of this.

I have a great appreciation for Thomas Paine, and his book *The Age of Reason* introduced me to deism. Then I discovered Matthew Tindal's book *Christianity as Old as Creation: or, the Gospel, a Republication of the Religion of*

Nature, which gave me an appreciation of deism as the ageless "Religion of Nature" consisting of honoring God by love for neighbor, as presented again in the "gospel" preached by Jesus. It was in Tindal's book that I became acquainted with the term "Christian Deist."

Matthew Tindal (165?-1733) was educated as a lawyer at Exeter College, Oxford University in England. Tindal earned three degrees and taught at All Soul's College, Oxford, from 1678 until his death in 1733. He was also an adviser to the English government on international law. Tindal was a Christian Deist but he was a member of the Church of England most of his life. Tindal's book was written in English but the book reflects Tindal's broad education in his frequent quotations in Latin and Greek from ancient philosophers and others.

Appendix Three concerns the Christian Deist Fellowship, a worldwide organization for persons who consider themselves to be Christian Deists. The Christian Deist Fellowship is not a church because Christian Deists do not have group worship of God. Christian Deism is a personal religion in which an individual worships (honors) God by living as God designed human beings to live, by loving (valuing) others as you love (value) yourself. The Christian Deist Fellowship provides an organization in which Christian Deists can claim membership when identifying their religion in response to anyone who may ask.

The Christian Deist Fellowship was legally organized March 12, 2009, under the Texas Unincorporated Nonprofit Association Act (Article 1396-70.01, Vernon's Texas Civil Statutes).

As stated in its Articles of Association, "the Fellowship is a religious organization whose members are bound by common beliefs, and it is formed to promote the principles and practice of Christian Deism. The Fellowship conducts

its mission through the internet and through voluntary
activities by individual members and local groups of
members."

APPENDIX ONE: THOMAS PAINE

Below, I am quoting excerpts from Thomas Paine's book *The Age of Reason* (Parts one and two) and then I am providing a commentary on Thomas Paine and his deism:

<u>QUOTATIONS FROM THOMAS PAINE'S BOOK, "THE AGE OF REASON"</u> (Sub-headings added):

1. <u>PAINE'S RELIGION</u>

I (Thomas Paine) believe in one God, and no more; and I hope for happiness beyond this life.

I believe in the equality of man; and I believe that religious duties consist of doing justice, loving mercy, and endeavoring to make our fellow creatures happy.

I do not believe in the creed professed by the Jewish Church, by the Roman Church, by the Greek Church, by the Turkish Church, by the Protestant Church, nor by any church that I know of. My own mind is my church.

All national institutions of churches, whether Jewish, Christian, or Turkish, appear to me no other than human inventions, set up to terrify and enslave mankind, and monopolize power and profit. (<u>Note from Brother John:</u> Thomas Paine used the term "Turkish" to refer to the religion of Islam, and Paine used the term "Christian" to refer to <u>trinitarian</u> Christianity.)

I (Thomas Paine) do not mean by this declaration to condemn those who believe otherwise; they have the same right to their belief as I have to mine. But it is necessary to the happiness of man that he be mentally faithful to himself. Infidelity does not consist of believing, or in disbelieving; it consists of professing to believe what he does not believe.

2. <u>GOD</u>

The only idea that man can affix to the name of God is that of a first cause, the cause of all things. And incomprehensible and difficult as it is for man to conceive what a first cause is, he arrives at the belief of it from the tenfold greater difficulty of disbelieving in it.

The existence of an Almighty Power is sufficiently demonstrated to us, though we cannot conceive, as it is impossible we should, the nature and manner of its existence. We cannot conceive how we came here ourselves, and yet we know for a fact that we are here.

. . . everything we behold carries in itself the internal evidence that it did not make itself. Every man is an evidence to himself he did not make himself; . . . neither could any tree, plant, or animal make itself; and it is the conviction arising from this evidence that carries us on, as it were, by necessity to the belief of a first cause eternally existing, of a nature totally different to any material existence that we know of, and by the power of which all things exist; and this first cause man calls God.

It is only by the exercise of reason that a man can discover God.

The Almighty Lecturer, by displaying the principles of science in the structure of the universe, has invited man to study and to imitation. It is as if He had said to the inhabitants of this globe that we call ours, 'I have made the earth for man to dwell upon, and I have rendered the starry heavens visible, to teach him science and the arts. He can now provide for his own comfort, and learn from my munificence to all, to be kind to each other.'

The true Deist has but one Deity, and his religion consists

in contemplating the power, wisdom, and benignity of the Deity in His works, and endeavoring to imitate Him in everything moral, scientific, and mechanical.

3. <u>JESUS</u>

Nothing that is here said can apply, even with the most distant disrespect, to the real character of Jesus Christ. He was a virtuous and amiable man. The morality he preached and practiced was of the most benevolent kind; and though similar systems of morality had been preached by Confucius, and by some Greek philosophers, many years before; and the Quakers since; and by many good men in all ages, it has not been exceeded by any.

That such a person as Jesus Christ existed, and that he was crucified, which was the mode of execution in that day, are historical relations strictly within the limits of probability. He preached most excellent morality and the equality of man, but he preached also against the corruptions and avarice of the Jewish priests, and this brought upon him the hatred and vengeance of the whole order of the priesthood.

The accusation which those priests brought against him was that of sedition and conspiracy against the Roman government, to which the Jews were then subject and tributary; and it is not improbable that the Roman government might have had some secret apprehensions of the effects of his doctrine, as well as the Jewish priests; neither improbable that Jesus Christ had in contemplation the delivery of the Jewish nation from the bondage of the Romans. Between the two, however, this virtuous reformer and revolutionist lost his life.

He was a Jew by birth and by profession; and he was the Son of God in the like manner that every person is--for the

Creator is Father of All.

4. TRINITARIAN CHRISTIANITY

But the belief of a God is a belief distinct from all other things, and ought not be confounded with any. The notion of the Trinity of Gods has enfeebled the belief in one God.

But when, according to the Christian Trinitarian scheme, one part of God is represented as a dying man, and another part, called the Holy Ghost, by a flying pigeon, it is impossible that belief can attach itself to such wild conceits.

Of all the systems of religion that ever were invented, there is none more derogatory to the Almighty, more unedifying to man, more repugnant to reason, and more contradictory to itself than this thing called Christianity. It is too absurd for belief, too impossible to convince, and too inconsistent to practice; it renders the heart torpid, or produces atheists and fanatics. As the engine of power, it serves the purpose of despotism; and as a means of wealth, the avarice of priests; but so far as respects the good of man, leads to nothing here or hereafter.
(Note from Brother John: Thomas Paine used the terms "Christianity" and "Christian" as defined by trinitarian churches, such as the Church of England and the Roman Catholic Church.)

5. TRINITARIAN DOCTRINE OF REDEMPTION

. . . hearing a sermon read by a relation of mine, who was a great devotee of the Church, upon the subject of what is called redemption by the death of the Son of God . . . I revolted at the recollection of what I heard, and thought to myself that it was making God Almighty act like a passionate man who killed his son when he could not

revenge himself in any other way, and as I was sure that a
man would he hanged who did such a thing, I could not
see for what purpose they preached such sermons.

. . . it was to me a serious reflection, arising from the idea I
had that God was too good to do such an action, and was
too almighty to be under any necessity of doing it. I believe
in the same manner at this moment; and I moreover
believe that any system of religion that has anything in it
that shocks the mind of a child cannot be a true system.

But the Christian story of God the Father putting his Son to
death, or employing people to do it, cannot be told by a
parent to a child; and to tell him that it was done to make
mankind happier and better is making the story still worse-
-as if mankind could be improved by the example of
murder; and to tell him that all of this is a mystery is only
making an excuse for the incredibility of it.

. . . moral justice cannot take the innocent for the guilty,
even if the innocent should offer itself. To suppose justice
to do this is to destroy the principle of its existence, which
is the thing itself; it is then no longer justice, it is
indiscriminate revenge.

6. WORD OF GOD

That the idea or belief of a Word of God existing in print, or
in writing, or in speech, is inconsistent in itself for reasons
already assigned. These reasons, among many others,
are the want of a universal language; the mutability of
language; the errors to which translations are subject; the
possibility of totally suppressing such a work; the
probability of altering it, or of fabricating the whole, and
imposing it on the world.

That the creation we behold is the real and ever-existing
Word of God, in which we cannot be deceived. It

proclaims His power, it demonstrates His wisdom, it manifests His goodness and beneficence.

It is only in the Creation that all our ideas and conceptions of a Word of God can unite. The creation speaks the universal language, independently of human speech or language, multiplied and various they be. It is an ever-existent original, which every man can read. It cannot be forged; it cannot be counterfeited; it cannot be lost; it cannot be altered; it cannot be suppressed. It does not depend upon the will of man whether it shall be published or not; it publishes itself from one end of the earth to the other. It preaches to all nations and to all worlds, and this Word of God reveals to man all that is necessary for man to know of God.

Do we want to contemplate His power? We see it in the immensity of the creation. Do we want to contemplate His wisdom? We see it in the unchangeable order by which the incomprehensible whole is governed. Do we want to contemplate His munificence? We see it in His not withholding that abundance even from the unthankful. In fine, do we want to know what God is? Search not the book called the Scripture, which any human hand might make, but a Scripture called creation.

The creation is the Bible of the Deist. He reads there, in the handwriting of the Creator himself, the certainty of His existence and the immutability of his power, and all other Bibles and Testaments are to him forgeries.

(<u>Note from Brother John:</u> In reference to the "Old Testament," which Thomas Paine called the "Bible," Paine wrote the following.)

Whenever we read the obscene stories, the voluptuous debaucheries, the cruel and torturous executions, the unrelenting vindictiveness, with which more than half the

Bible is filled, it would be more consistent that we call it the word of a demon than the Word of God. It is a history of wickedness that has served to corrupt and brutalize mankind; and for my part, I sincerely detest everything that is cruel.

(<u>Note from Brother John:</u> In reference to the "New Testament," Thomas Paine wrote the following.)

Had it been the object or intention of Jesus Christ to establish a new religion, he would undoubtably have written the system himself, or procured it to be written in his life-time. But there is no publication extant authenticated with his name. All of the books called the New Testament were written after his death.

Jesus Christ founded no new system. He called men to the practice of moral virtues and to the belief in one God.

7. <u>MIRACLES</u>

Of all the modes of evidence that ever were invented to obtain belief in any system of opinion to which the name of religion has been given, that of miracle, however successful the imposition may have been, is the most inconsistent. For, in the first place, whenever recourse is had to show, for the purpose of procuring that belief (for miracle, under any idea of the word, is a show), it implies a lameness or weakness in the doctrine that is preached.

In every point of view in which those things called miracles can be placed or considered, the reality of them is improbable and their existence unnecessary. . . .it is more difficult to obtain belief to a miracle than to a principle evidently moral without a miracle.

8. PROPHECIES

. . . the flights and metaphors of the Jewish poets, and phrases and expressions now rendered obscure by our not being acquainted with the local circumstances to which they applied at the time they were used, have been erected as prophecies and made to bend to explanations at the will and whimsical conceits of the sectaries, expounders and commentators.

9. MORALITY

Were a man impressed as fully and as strongly as he ought to be with the belief of a God, his moral life would be regulated by the force of that belief; he would stand in awe of God and himself, and would not do a thing that could not be concealed from either.

.The moral duty of man consists in imitating the moral goodness and beneficence of God, manifested in the creation toward all of His creatures. That seeing, as we daily do, the goodness of God to all men, it is an example calling upon all men to practice the same toward each other, and consequently, that everything of persecution and revenge between man and man, and everything of cruelty to animals, is a violation of moral duty.

10. REVELATION

But though, speaking for myself, I admit the possibility of revelation, I totally disbelieve that the Almighty ever did communicate anything to man, by any mode of speech, in any language, by any kind of vision, or appearance, or by any means which our senses are capable of receiving, otherwise than the universal display of Himself in the works of creation, and by the repugnance we feel in ourselves in bad actions, and the disposition to do good ones.

If we consider the nature of our condition here, we must see there is no occasion for such a thing as revealed religion. What is it we want to know? Does not the creation, the universe we behold, preach to us the existence of an Almighty Power that governs and regulates the whole? And is not the evidence that creation holds out to our senses infinitely stronger than anything we can read in a book that any imposter might make and call the Word of God? As for morality, the knowledge of it exists in every man's conscience.

11. HEREAFTER

I trouble not myself about the manner of future existence. I content myself with believing, even to positive conviction, that the Power that gave me existence is able to continue it, in any form or manner He pleases, either with or without a body, and it appears more probable that I shall continue to exist hereafter, than that I should have had existence, as I now have, before that existence began.

We must know that the Power that called us into being can, if He pleases, and when He pleases, call us to account for the manner in which we have lived here; and therefore without seeking any other motive for the belief, it is rational to believe that He will, for we know beforehand that He can. The probability, or even the possibility of the thing is all that we ought to know;

The probability that we may be called to account hereafter will, to the reflecting mind, have the influence of belief; . . . As this is the state we are in, and it is proper that we should be in, as free agents, it is the fool only . . . that would live as if there were no God.

Thomas Paine, like all deists, believed that all of creation reflects the existence of a Creator, called God. Paine wrote, ". . . everything we behold carries in itself the internal evidence that it did not make itself. Every man is an evidence to himself that he did not make himself . . . neither could any tree, plant, or animal make itself; and it is from the conviction rising from this evidence that carries us on, as it were, by necessity of belief of a first cause eternally existing, of a nature totally different from any material existence we know of, and by the power of which all things exist; and this first cause man calls God."

Paine believed that "we cannot conceive the nature and manner of its (God's) existence" but the belief in God's existence is sufficient to guide a person in his or her behavior. Paine wrote, "Were man impressed as fully and as strongly as he ought to be with the belief of a God, his moral life would be regulated by the force of that belief; he would stand in awe of God and himself, and would not do a thing that could not be concealed from either. To give this belief the full opportunity of force, it is necessary that it act alone." Paine wrote, "We must know that the Power that called us into being can, if He pleases, and when He pleases, call us to account for the manner in which we have lived here, and, therefore without seeking any other motive for the belief, it is rational to believe that He will, for we know beforehand that He can. The probability, or even the possibility of a thing is all that we ought to know." Paine concluded, "It is the fool only who would live as if there were no God."

Although Paine believed that "everything we behold" evidences the existence of God, Paine was especially impressed with what he believed about the universe. In his "Discourse on the Existence of God," which Paine gave to the Theophilanthropist Society in 1797, Paine expressed his belief that motion provided by God kept the planets in orbit to prevent their destruction. In this lecture, Paine claimed that motion (orbiting) was not a property of matter (the planets) and, therefore, this motion is evidence of God's existence.

The Theophilanthropist Society in France was Thomas Paine's effort to organize deism, as Paine viewed it.

The Theophilanthropist Society was created on the basis of a 60 page <u>Manual of the Theophilanthropes</u> which Paine wrote in 1796 and published in September of that year. In his "Precise History of the Theophilanthropists," Paine wrote that "The society takes the name Theophilanthropes, which would be rendered in English by the word Theophilanthopists, a word compounded of three Greek words, signifying God, Love, and Man. The explanation of this word is, Lovers of God and Man, or Adorers of God and Friends of Man." According to Paine, "The principles of the Theophilanthropists are the same as those published the first part of <u>The Age of Reason</u> in 1793**, and in the second part in 1795." (<u>Note from Brother John</u>: The first part was written in 1793 but published in 1794.)

In 1797, five families of Theophilanthropists, in Paris, France, organized the first society of Theophilanthopists. Paine wrote, "The care of conducting this society was undertaken by the five fathers of the families. They adopted the Manual of the Theophilanthropists. They agreed to hold their days of public worship on days corresponding to Sundays but without making this a hindrance to other societies to choose such other day as they thought convenient. Soon after this, other societies were opened, of which some celebrate on the decadi (tenth day) and others on the Sunday: it was also resolved that the committee should meet one hour each week for the purpose of preparing or examining discourses and lectures for the next general assembly."

Paine wrote, "The society proposes to publish each year a volume entitled Year religious of the Theophilanthropists . . . Being a collection of discourses, lectures, hymns, and canticles, for all religious and moral festivals of the Theophilanthropists, whether in their public temples or in their private families, published by the author** of the Manual of the Theophilanthropists" (**Note: who, of course, was Thomas Paine). Paine wrote that the first volume of the <u>Religious Year of the Theophilanthropists</u> contained 214 pages and "The following is the table of contents:"

"1. Precise History of the Theophilanthropists.** (**Note: This was written by Thomas Paine)
 2. Exercises common to all Festivals.
 3. Hymn No. I God of whom the universe speaks..
 4. Discourse upon the existence of God.** (**Note: This was given by Thomas Paine)
 5. Ode II. The heavens instruct the earth.
 6. Precepts of Wisdom, extracted from the book of the Adorateurs
 7. Canticle, III. God Creator, soul of nature.
 8, Extracts from divers moralists upon the nature of God, and upon the physical proofs of his existence.
 9. Canticle, IV. Let us bless at our waking the God who gives us light.
10, Moral thoughts extracted from the Bible.
11. Hymn, No. V Father of the universe.
12, Contemplation of nature on the first days of spring.
13. Ode, No. VI Lord in thy glory adorable.
14, Extracts from the moral thoughts of Confucius
15. Canticle in praise of actions, and thanks for the works of creation.

16. Continuation from the moral thoughts of Confucius.
17. Hymn, No. VII All the universe is full of thy magnificence.
18. Extracts from an ancient sage of India upon the duties of families.
19. Upon the Spring.
20. Moral thoughts of divers Chinese authors. Canticle, No. VIII Everything celebrates the glory of the eternal.
21. Continuation of the moral thought of Chinese authors.
22. Invocation for the country.
24, Extracts from the moral thoughts of Theognis.
25. Invocation. Creator of man.
26. Ode, No. IX. Upon death.
27. Extracts from the book of the Moral Universe, upon happiness.
28. Ode, No. X. Supreme Author of Nature.

In his "Precise History of the Theophilanthropists," Paine wrote, "That the general assemblies should be called fetes (festivals) religious and moral. That those festivals should be conducted, in principle and form, in a manner so as not to be considered as festivals of an exclusive worship, and that, in recalling those who might be attached to any particular worship, those festivals might be attended as moral exercises by the disciples of every sect, and consequently avoid, by scrupulous care, everything that might make the society appear under the name of a sect. The society adopts neither rites nor priesthood, and it will never lose sight of the resolution not to advance anything, as a society, inconvenient to any sect or sects, in any time or country, and under any government."

Paine did not want the Theophilanthropists to appear to be a "sect," and their public assemblies were open to persons of all "sects," but the Theophilanthropist Societies had characteristics of a "church," such as "public worship" in "public temples." When the Catholic church was outlawed by the revolutionary government in France, ten of the parish church buildings were provided to the

Theophilanthropists for their assemblies. These public assemblies included "hymns, Odes, and Canticles" regarding God, as usually found in public worship in churches. Although the Theophilanthropists had "neither rites nor priesthood," their "public worship" was contrary to the basic deist belief that worship of God is a private matter, and is done by living as God designed human beings to live.

Paine wrote, "The Theohilanthropists do not call themselves the disciples of such or such a man. They avail themselves of the precepts that have been transmitted by writers of all countries and in all ages . . . Next follow the dogmas of the Theophilanthropists, or things they profess to believe. These are two, and they are thus expressed: The Theophilanthropists believe in the existence of God, and the immortality of the soul."

In his view of deism, Paine claimed that belief in the "the existence of God" and belief in "the immortality of the soul" are essential "dogmas." These two claims call for examination.

Paine wrote, "Were a man impressed as fully and as strongly as he ought to be with the belief of a God, his moral life would be regulated by the force of this belief; he would stand in awe of God and himself, and would not do a thing that could not be concealed from either. To give this belief the full opportunity of force, it is necessary that if act alone. And this is Deism." Paine thought that belief in the existence of God, by itself, is enough to regulate a person's behavior because "We must know that the Power that called us into existence . . . can call us to account for the manner in which we have lived here."

Thomas Paine's view that person's "moral life" is determined by a person's "belief in the existence of God" is simply NOT TRUE. We see persons express their belief in the "existence of God" by shouting "Allah is great" but they fly airplanes into office buildings, murdering thousands of people, a most immoral act (This refers to the September 11, 2001, attack on the World Trade Center in New York). We also see persons, called "atheists," who do not believe in the "existence of God" but they are good people who live moral lives.

Deists do believe in the existence of God but do not make this belief essential in determining how human beings ought to live. Deists agree with Paine that God communicates with us "by the repugnance we feel in ourselves in bad actions and the disposition to do good ones." Deists believe that this "disposition" to do good is inherent in the design of human nature, whether or not a person professes a belief in the "existence" of God. Deists believe that from our own human nature, experience, and reasoning, we can know how we ought to live.

It is natural for a person to love (value) oneself, so any action that is hurtful or uncaring to oneself is instinctively, or naturally, known to be "wrong." Using one's own power of reasoning (rational thinking), a person knows that a hurtful or uncaring action toward another person is also "wrong." This logical way of thinking has produced a universal guide for personal behavior, "Treat others as you would have others treat you" (the "Golden Rule). This was expressed by a man named Jesus of Nazareth in "Love your neighbor as (you love) yourself" (Matthew 22:39) and "Whatever (good) you wish that others would do to you, do so unto them" (Matthew 7:12).

Jesus taught these concepts in his parable of "the Good Samaritan" (Luke 10:30-37). In this story, we see the "hurtful" actions of the robbers who beat and robbed a man, the "uncaring" actions of the priest and Levite who ignored the suffering of the beaten man, and the "loving" actions of the Samaritan who took care of the beaten man.

"Hurtful" actions that cause human suffering, and "uncaring" actions that are indifferent to human suffering are two kinds of "wrong" (called "sin.").

Deists believe that human beings know that they are designed to do good to each other because this brings feelings of self-approval. Dr. Thomas Young, an early American deist, expressed it this way, "I believe, that in the order of nature and providence, the man who most assiduously endeavors to promote the will of God in the good of his fellow creatures, receives the most simple reward of his virtue, the peace of mind and silent applause of a good conscience, which administers more solid satisfaction than all of the other enjoyments of life put together."

Thomas Paine claimed that belief in the "immortality of the soul" is a "dogma" in what Paine called "Theophilanthropism." We do not know what Paine exactly meant by "immortality of the soul." But it appears that Paine believed that a person continues to exist after one's present life because Paine wrote, "I content myself with believing, even with positive conviction, that the Power that gave me existence is able to continue it, in any form or manner He pleases, with or without a body, and it appears more probable that I shall continue hereafter than that I should have had existence, as I now have, before that existence began." Paine also wrote, "We must know that the Power that called us into being can . . . call us to account for the manner in which we have lived here."

Deists agree that from the existence of life we have now, we can infer that a Life-giver has the power to give life, but there is no reason to believe that that an individual's present life "continues" in a "hereafter" so God can "call us to account for the manner in which we have lived here," as Paine believed. Some religions use belief in a "hereafter" to threaten unending punishment in "hell" for persons who do not accept those religions. Deists reject those religions that are based on fear of punishment in a "hereafter."

Deists believe that God designed human beings to care for each other. A person who lives in this way enjoys the personal satisfaction that comes now from being a loving person, and has reason to hope for another life from God. (Note: This does not necessarily mean that an individual's present identity will "continue" after one's present life. A future life may mean a new beginning with a new personal identity.)

When General Napoleon Bonaparte became Emperor of France, he restored the Catholic Church, and Theophilanthropist Societies disappeared in France. Upon Paine's return to the United States, he tried to establish a Theophilanthopist Society but this did not succeed. Deism is a religion but it does not have public worship as Paine proposed for the Theophilanthropist Society. (<u>Note from Brother John</u>: In my view, deists can benefit from fellowship with each other, but public worship is contrary to a basic principle in deism: Deists, as individuals, worship (show respect for) God by trying to live as God designed us to live, by love for each other, and by repenting if we fail to love.

APPENDIX TWO: MATTHEW TINDAL

Thomas Paine's book *The Age of Reason* (parts one and two) has been helpful to me and I have much admiration for Thomas Paine, but I found a deeper understanding of deism from another book, *Christianity as Old as Creation* (1730) by Matthew Tindal who introduced me to "Christian deism." I am providing excerpts from Tindal's book below, and then I am providing a commentary on Matthew Tindal and his deism.

QUOTATIONS FROM MATTHEW TINDAL'S BOOK, "CHRISTIANITY AS OLD AS CREATION, or, THE GOSPEL, A REPUBLICATION OF THE RELIGION OF NATURE" (Note: the numbering of these excerpts and the underlining have been added.)

1. "True Christianity is not a Religion of Yesterday, but what God, at the Beginning, dictated and still continues to dictate to Christians, as well as others.

2 "Christianity, tho' the Name is of a later Date, must be as old, and extensive, as human Nature; and the Law of our Creation, must have been implanted in us by God himself.

3. "All men, at all times, must have sufficient Means to discover whatever God designs (us) to know, and practice.

4. "If God designed Mankind should know, believe, profess, and practice, and has given them no other Means for this, but the Use of Reason; Reason, human reason must then be that Means: For as God has made us that 'tis Will, that we act up to the Dignity of our Nature; so 'tis Reason must tell us when we do so." By Natural Religion, I understand the Belief in the existence of God, and the Sense and Practice of those Duties which result from the

Knowledge we, by our Reason, have of him and his Perfections; and us and our Imperfections; and of the relation we stand in to him and our Fellow Creatures; so that the Religion of Nature takes in everything that is founded on the Reason and Nature of things.

5.   "Our Reason, which gives us a Demonstration of the divine Perfections, affords us the same concerning the Nature of those Duties which God requires, not only in relation to himself, but to ourselves, and to one another. These we can't but see, if we look into ourselves, consider our own Natures, and the Circumstances God placed us in with relation to our Fellow- Creatures, and what conduces to our mutual Happiness: Our Senses, our Reason, the experiences of others and our own, can't fail to give us sufficient Information.

6.   "All moralists agree, that human Nature is so constituted, that Men can't live without Society and mutual Assistance; and that God has endowed them with Reason, Speech, and other Faculties, evidently fitted to enable them to assist each other in all the Concerns of Life, that, therefore, 'tis the Will of God who gives them this Nature, and endows them with these Faculties, that they should employ them to their common Benefit and mutual assistance.

7.   "In a word, as a most beneficent Disposition in the supreme Being is the Source of all his Actions in relation to his Creatures; so he has implanted in Man, whom he has made after his own Image, a Love for his Species; the gratifying of which, in doing Acts of Benevolence, Compassion, and Good Will, produces Pleasures that never satiates; as on the contrary, Actions of Ill-Nature, Envy, Malice, etc. never fail to produce Shame, Confusion, and everlasting Self-Reproach.

8.   "Hence, I think, we may define True Religion to consist

of the constant Disposition of Mind to do all the Good we can; and thereby render ourselves acceptable to God in answering the End of our Creation.

9.   "I think, we may conclude, that Men, according as they do, or do not partake of the Nature of God, must unavoidably be happy, or miserable. And herein appear the great Wisdom of God, in making Mens Misery or Happiness the necessary and inseparable Consequences of Actions; and their rational Actions carry with them their own Reward, and irrational (Actions) their own Punishment.

10. "As it was for the sake of Man that God gave him Laws, so God executes them purely for the same reason; since on God's own account, God can't be the least affected, whether his Laws be or not observed; and consequently in punishing, no more in rewarding, does God act as a Party, much less as an injured Party, who wants Satisfaction, or Reparation of Honor. And indeed, to suppose it, is highly to dishonor God, since God, as he can never be injured, so he can never want Reparation;

11. "All Punishment for Punishment's sake is mere Cruelty and Malice, which can never be in God; nor can God hate anything God has made, or be subject to such Weakness or Impotence as to act arbitrarily, or out of Spite, Wrath, Revenge or any Self-interest; and consequently, whatever Punishment God inflicts, must be a Mark of his Love, in not suffering (allowing) his Creatures to remain in that miserable State, which is inseparable from Sin and Wickedness.

12.   "By the Law of Nature a well as the Gospel, the Honor of God, and the Good of Man, being the two grand or general Commandments; all particular Precepts must be comprehended under these two, and being alike to the Law of Nature as well as the Gospel; and what does not,

can belong to neither.

"These two grand Laws are in effect the same, since what promotes the Honour of God necessarily promotes the Good of Man. The more we love and honor God, the more we shall imitate him in our extensive Love to our Fellow-Creatures, who are equally Children of God.

13.   "The Religion of the Gospel is the Original Religion of Reason and Nature -- That the Doctrine of Repentance, with which the Gospel set out in the World, and had reference to the Law of Reason and Nature, against which Men had everywhere offended, and since Repentance infers the Necessity of future Reformation, and Return to that Duty and Obedience, from which we are fallen; the Consequence is manifestly this, that the Gospel was a Republication of the Law of Nature, and its Precepts declarative of that Original Religion, which was as Old as Creation." (Note: Matthew Tindal quoted this paragraph from a sermon by Dr. Sherlock, then Bishop of Bangor. The title of Tindal's book, Christianity as Old as Creation,_ or, the Gospel a Republication of the Religion of Nature is based on this paragraph from Dr. Sherlock's sermon.)

14. "Christian Deists own . . . that the necessary Relation that is between Things, makes some Actions moral, and others immoral . . . but conclude, that those which evidently tend to promote Honour of God and the Practice of Righteousness, are plain moral Duties, and perpetually oblige.

LINDELL'S COMMENTARY ON TINDAL

Thomas Paine's book, *The Age of Reason*, introduced me to deism, but it was Matthew Tindal's book that gave me a fuller understanding of deism.

Deists believe that all human beings, "at all times, must have had sufficient means to discover whatever God designed they should know and practice" (Excerpt No. 3, above), and the means for this are God-given power of reason (rational thinking) and the design of human nature.

According to excerpt No. 6 above, "if we look into ourselves, consider our own natures, and the circumstances God has placed us in with relation to our fellow-creatures, and what conduces to our mutual happiness, our senses, our reason, the experiences of others and our own, give us sufficient information concerning those duties which God requires, not only in relation to God, but to ourselves, and to one another."

This is a classic statement of the basic deist belief that through (1) <u>senses</u> (sight, hearing, touch, taste, smell) by which we perceive ourselves and our surroundings, (2) <u>experiences</u> (what happens to us and others), and (3) <u>reason</u> (rational thinking) by which we evaluate perceptions and experiences, we have "sufficient information" to know "those duties which God requires, not only in relation to God, but to ourselves, and to one another." Tindal wrote, "that human nature is so constituted that human beings cannot live without Society and mutual Assistance, and that God has endowed them with Reason, Speech, and other Faculties, evidently fitted to enable them to assist each other in all the Concerns of Life; that, therefore, 'tis the Will of God who gives them this Nature, and endows them with these Faculties, that they should employ them to their common benefit and mutual assistance." (Excerpt No.7).

Deists believe that human beings have "free will," the power to choose their actions. Since God has "implanted in Man . . . a Love for his Species" (Excerpt No. 8), we know when "we act up to the Dignity of our Natures; so 'tis Reason must tell us when we do so." (Excerpt No. 4)

Tindal wrote, "And herein appears the great Wisdom of God, in making Men's Misery or Happiness the necessary and inseparable Consequences of Actions; and their rational Actions carry with them their own Reward, and irrational (actions) their own Punishment." (Excerpt No. 10)   "Doing acts of Benevolence, Compassion, and Good Will produces Pleasures that never satiates; as on the contrary, Actions of Ill-Nature, Envy, Malice, etc. never fail to produce Shame, Confusion, and everlasting Self-Reproach." (Excerpt No. 8)

Tindal believed that the "Law of Nature" and the (Christian) "Gospel" both include "the Honour of God, and the Good of Man." Tindal wrote, "These two grand laws are in effect the same, since what promotes the Honour of God necessarily promotes the Good of Man." (Excerpt No 13). "Hence, I think, we may define True Religion to consist in the constant Disposition of Mind to do all the good we can; and thereby render ourselves acceptable to God in answering the End of our Creation." (Excerpt No. 9) This is a basic belief in deism: We honor God by doing good to each other, as we are naturally designed to do.

Tindal obviously recognized the "two grand laws" ("Honor of God and the Good of Man") in the "gospel" of Jesus, "You shall love the Lord your God with all your heart, and with all your soul, and with all your mind. This is the greatest commandment. And the second is like it: You shall love your neighbor as yourself." (Matthew: 22:37-39)

Tindal wrote, "By the Law of Nature as well as the Gospel,

the Honour of God, and the Good of Man, being the two grand or general Commandments; all particular Precepts must be comprehended under these two, and being alike to the Law of Nature as well as the Gospel; and what does not, can belong to neither." (Excerpt No. 13) (In Matthew 22:40, too)

Tindal rejected the church doctrine that Jesus died to satisfy a death penalty imposed by God on mankind because of their disobedience. Tindal wrote, "As it was for the sake of Man that God gave him Laws, so God executes them purely for the same reason; since on God's account, God can't be the least affected, whether his Laws be, or not be observed; and consequently in punishing, no more than in rewarding, does God act as a Party, much less as an injured Party, who wants Satisfaction, or Reparation of Honor. And indeed, to suppose it, is highly to dishonor God, since God, as he can never be injured, so he can never want Reparation;"

Tindal wrote that "Men's Misery or Happiness (are) the necessary and inseparable Consequences of Actions; and their rational (good) actions carry with them their own Reward, and irrational (bad actions) their own punishment." (Excerpt 10.) Tindal believed that a person is punished for bad actions by the misery that a person feels from "shame, confusion, and self- reproach" but this punishment is intended to bring that person to repentance and reformation. Tindal wrote that God cannot act "out of Spite, Wrath, Revenge or any Self-interest; and consequently, whatever Punishment God inflicts must be a mark of his Love, in not suffering (allowing) his Creatures to remain in that miserable State, which is inseparable from Sin and Wickedness." (Excerpt No. 12)

Tindal quoted from a sermon by Dr. Sherlock, then Bishop of Bangor, "The Religion of the Gospel is the true Original Religion of Reason and Nature -- That the Doctrine of

Repentance, with which the Gospel set out in the World, and had reference to the Law of Reason and Nature, against which Men had everywhere offended; and since Repentance infers the Necessity of a future Reformation, and a Return to Duty and Obedience, from which, by Transgression, we are fallen; the Consequence is manifestly this, that the Gospel was a Republication of the Law of Nature, and its Precepts declarative of that Original Religion, which was as Old as Creation."

The title of Tindal's book, *Christianity as Old as Creation, or, The Gospel, a Republication of the Religion of Nature* comes mostly from Dr. Sherlock's words. Tindal views the essence of the "Religion of Nature" and the Christian "Gospel" as one and the same: We honor God by doing good to each other. Tindal uses the term "Christian Deist." in his book (Excerpt No. 15).

APPENDIX THREE: CHRISTIAN DEIST FELLOWSHIP

The Christian Deist Fellowship was created as an Unincorporated Nonprofit Association on March 12, 2009 under laws of the State of Texas (Texas Uniform Unincorporated Nonprofit Association Act, Article 1396-70.01, Vernon's Texas Civil Statutes). One purpose of this Association is to provide an organization in which individual Christian Deists may claim membership when identifying his or her personal religious affiliation.

Below are the Constitution and By-Laws of the Christian Deist Fellowship. The Constitution contains a brief statement of beliefs by which a person can determine whether he or she belongs to the Christian Deist Fellowship. Membership in the Fellowship is immediate for anyone who identifies himself or herself as a member. No application or registration is required.

Article 1: Name of organization
Christian Deist Fellowship

Article 2: Purpose

To provide an organization for Christian Deists and to promote the practice of Christian Deism through free educational and religious activities.

Article 3: Membership
All individuals who identify themselves as Christian Deists are members of the Christian Deist Fellowship. A Christian Deist believes:

1. Jesus was a man who worshiped God, our Creator.

2. Jesus taught that it is God's will for you to "love

your neighbor (including enemies) as yourself" (Matthew 22:39; 5:43-44) which means that "whatever you wish that people would do to you, do so to them" (Matthew 7:12).

3. God's will is taught to everyone by God (John 6:45) in the design of human nature, and is learned through human experience and reasoning. We worship (honor) God by doing God's will.

4. Failures to love others, by causing human suffering or by being indifferent to human suffering, are offenses (sins) against God, and are destructive to your soul (inner self, or life).

5. If you repent of your sins and forgive others who sin against you, God forgives your sins (Matthew 6:14-15) and restores your soul.

6. If you try to live by love for others, and sincerely repent of your failures to love, you will enjoy satisfaction with yourself in this life, and you have reason to hope that God will give you another life.

Article 4: Offices

The Christian Deist Fellowship is an egalitarian organization so all members are of equal rank and are authorized to serve as official representatives of the Christian Deist Fellowship to provide religious, educational, and humanitarian services to other people free and without charge, including performance of marriage ceremonies in accord with State laws.

Article 5: Finance

The Christian Deist Fellowship has no financial assets or property, and no monetary income.

Article 6: Meetings
The Christian Deist Fellowship has no regular meetings.
Members may meet in local groups for the purpose of
social fellowship, religious education, and humanitarian
activities but Christian Deists do not have public worship
services.

Article 7: Amendments

This constitution and bylaws may be amended by a
majority vote of the members of the Christian Deist
Fellowship in an election advertised and conducted on the
internet.

Article 8: Dissolution of Organization

The Christian Deist Fellowship shall exist in perpetuity unless
dissolved by a two-thirds (2/3) vote of the members of the
Christian Deist Fellowship in an election advertised and
conducted on the internet.

Article 9: Initial Agent and Headquarters Location

The initial agent for the Christian Deist Fellowship is
Brother John Lindell, founder of the Christian Deism
website (The Human Jesus and Christian Deism), and the
initial headquarters location is his residence in Travis
County, Texas.

www.ingramcontent.com/pod-product-compliance
Lightning Source LLC
Chambersburg PA
CBHW072010150726
47999CB00002B/594